McGraw-Hill's

TABE

Tests of Adult Basic Education

Level A

Mathematics Workbook

McGraw-Hill's
TABE

Tests of Adult Basic Education

Level A
Mathematics Workbook

Richard Ku

New York   Chicago   San Francisco   Lisbon   London   Madrid
Mexico City   Milan   New Delhi   San Juan   Seoul   Singapore
Sydney   Toronto

CONTENTS

INTRODUCTION

The purpose of this workbook is to assist you in preparing for the mathematics portions of the TABE Level A Test. The book seeks to help you

- Identify gaps in your skills and your understanding of mathematics concepts.
- Fill those gaps with explanations, examples, and practice problems.

There are two math parts of the TABE Level A:

- The *Math Computation* section assesses your math skills without the use of a calculator.
- The *Applied Math* section assesses your ability to apply math concepts by solving a variety of real-world problems with the use of a calculator.

Each of these parts comes in a Survey (short) form and a Complete Battery (long) form. Both the Pretest and the Posttest in this book are Complete Battery forms. The Math Computation section consists of 40 problems to be completed in 24 minutes. The Applied Math section consists of 50 problems to be completed in 50 minutes.

How This Book Is Organized

A Pretest and its answer key follow this introductory chapter. The goal of the Pretest is to help you identify your weaknesses. Use the Pretest answer key to determine which problems you got wrong, and find the lessons where these problems are covered.

The first six lessons after the Pretest cover topics in the Math Computation part of the test:

1. Decimals
2. Fractions
3. Integers
4. Percent
5. Operations
6. Algebra

Since you are preparing for the Level A test, it is assumed that you've mastered whole number arithmetic, and there are no lessons on these topics.

The second six lessons cover topics in the Applied Math section of the test:

7. Problem Solving
8. Applied Algebra
9. Geometry
10. Measurement
11. Coordinate Geometry
12. Data Analysis

These 12 lessons include examples and practice problems for every type of problem described in the book.

A Posttest and its answer key follow the 12 lessons. The book ends with an appendix that provides answer explanations to all Pretest and Posttest questions and to all practice problems in the lessons.

Taking the Pretest

Your first task after you finish reading this introduction is to take the Pretest. At a minimum, you should take each part without interruption. You have 24 minutes for the Math Computation part and 50 minutes for the Applied Math part. You should allow 15 minutes to score each part and mark the errors. It will take about an hour and a half to take and score both parts of the Pretest. It may be a better idea for you to take and score the two parts at separate times. For each question you get wrong, **highlight** the corresponding topic and lesson shown in the answer key. This will make it easy to find the lesson you need to study.

Using the Lessons

The lessons that follow the Pretest are organized into topics that correspond to questions in the TABE Level A. Much of the material in these lessons will be familiar to you. Each lesson begins with a brief description of what the topic is about and the meanings of key words and phrases. These words and phrases are written in **boldface**. Math is more than just numbers. You need to understand the language used to describe the properties of numbers and their relationships.

This verbal aspect of math is especially important for taking tests. You need to be sure you understand *what* a problem is asking you to find or do. Once the meaning of a problem is clear, you may discover that you already know *how* to do the problem. Read the examples in the lessons clearly and concentrate on the way problems are worded. Familiarize yourself with the meanings of questions. Understanding the meaning of a question is half the battle.

Important points are highlighted in the lessons by the use of bullets. A bulleted passage is often a restatement of a point made earlier, sometimes using different words.

Practice problems are provided for each section of a lesson.[1] These are exactly what their name means: **practice**. Learning math skills is just like learning to play a sport or a musical instrument. You may understand the principle, but you need practice to improve your skill level.

At a minimum, you should study each lesson that goes with a Pretest problem you got wrong. You should allow yourself at least an hour to read each lesson, try the practice problems, and check the solutions and answers. Some chapters may take more time. Since abstract explanations may be difficult to follow at times, the lessons use several examples to illustrate the main ideas. Take your time to understand how the examples illustrate the lesson description. Use similar situations you have experienced to reinforce lesson ideas, especially in the Applied Math part.

Answers and explanations to practice problems are in the appendix at the end of this book. Be sure to look at these solutions when checking your answers to the exercises. Try to be clear about your errors on problems you got wrong. Understanding why an answer is wrong is the most important part of the learning process.

If you have time, you should browse through the other lessons just to remind yourself of what topics you might see on the test. It would probably be a good idea to try an exercise or two from each section of these lessons just to build your confidence.

Taking the Posttest

When you've finished studying the lessons, take the Posttest. The purpose of this test is to see how well you've learned what you needed to learn. Questions in the Posttest are similar to those in the Pretest—no easier and no harder. The length and format of the Posttest is identical to the Pretest: a Math Computation part with 40 questions and an Applied Math part with 50 questions. Take each part (or both together) without interruption—under test conditions.

Use the answer key to get your score. As with the Pretest, the answer key to the Posttest cross-references the lesson topics. You might have to attain a certain score to qualify for a program. If your Posttest score is lower than this, restudy the lessons for the problems you got wrong; wait a week; and take each part of the Posttest again.

Whatever your immediate objective (such as achieving a certain score on the test), the result of any learning experience should contribute toward the larger goal of lifetime learning. The effort you put into preparing for the TABE Level A math tests should provide a benefit that goes beyond your score on this test.

---

[1] The section on "Data Presentation" in Lesson 12 contains several examples, but no exercises. Excellent tables, charts, and graphs can be found in newspapers and magazines.

Testing Tips

Both parts of the TABE Level A math test are multiple choice. All of the questions on the Math Computation part have four answer choices and a fifth choice called "None of these." Questions on the Applied Math part all have four answer choices, one of which is correct.

Try to resist the temptation to guess the correct answer choice on a multiple-choice test. It is generally best to work out the answer using methods described in this book. Hopefully, your answer will be one of the answer choices. If it's not, don't be too hasty to select "None of these" as your choice. First check your work to see if you made a careless mistake. Then check to see that your answer is an answer to the question being asked. For example, in a question that asks about a discount, you need to know whether the question asks you to determine the "amount of the discount" or the "discounted amount."

Don't allow yourself to get stuck on a question. If you can't "match" an answer choice after following the suggestions of the previous paragraph, move on to another question. You can always return to the one you got stuck on if there's time left after you've finished trying all the questions.

Calculators

The use of a calculator is permitted on the Applied Math part of the test. Over the years, calculators have become more powerful and less expensive. While you may be able to get a basic four-function (add, subtract, multiply, and divide) calculator for free, you should consider spending $10 to $15 to buy a scientific calculator. Some of these even have the capability of doing arithmetic with fractions and giving a fractional answer. They have grouping symbols (parentheses) and follow the order of operations. It is very easy to do a lengthy calculation at once instead of performing one operation at a time and writing intermediate answers on paper. Finally, it will be a valuable resource should you pursue your General Educational Development (GED) credential or other further education.

Whatever type of calculator you decide to use, be sure to spend time learning its main features. Newer calculators are quite user-friendly, and the manuals and reference cards that come with them are easy to follow. The worst thing you can do is "borrow" a calculator you've never used on the way to a test!

McGraw-Hill's

TABE

Tests of Adult Basic Education

Level A

Mathematics Workbook

Pretest

PART I: Mathematics Computation
Note: No calculator permitted

Date: _____   **Start Time:** _____

1. $8.23 - 5.06$

   A   3.27

   B   3.63

   C   2.37

   D   3.17

   E   None of these

2. $^-35 \div 7$

   A $^-5$

   B   5

   C $^-6$

   D   6

   E   None of these

3. $6\frac{7}{8} + 3\frac{1}{8} =$

   A   10

   B $9\frac{8}{16}$

   C $10\frac{5}{8}$

   D $3\frac{3}{4}$

   E   None of these

4. Solve for x: $x + 3 = 7$

   A   10

   B   21

   C   4

   D   5

   E   None of these

5. 10% of 500 =

   A   50

   B   5

   C   490

   D   5000

   E   None of these

6. $\sqrt{100} =$

   A   50

   B   25

   C   9

   D   10

   E   None of these

7. $^-13 + 6 =$

    A $^-19$

    B $^-7$

    C   19

    D   7

    E   None of these

8. $0.22 - 0.107 =$

    A   0.85

    B   0.113

    C   0.129

    D   0.127

    E   None of these

9.
$$6\frac{1}{2}$$
$$-\ 3\frac{1}{3}$$
$$\overline{}$$

    A $3\frac{1}{6}$

    B $9\frac{2}{5}$

    C $2\frac{1}{6}$

    D $3\frac{1}{3}$

    E   None of these

10. $2^2 + 3^2 =$

    A   25

    B   13

    C   36

    D   10

    E   None of these

11. $38.4 + 0.321 =$

    A   0.63

    B   3.529

    C   38.721

    D   41.61

    E   None of these

12. $7 + {}^-5 + {}^-3 =$

    A   15

    B $^-1$

    C   1

    D $^-15$

    E   None of these

13. $2.74 \times 10^{-3} =$

    A   2740

    B   274

    C   0.274

    D   0.00274

    E   None of these

14. $0 - 9 =$

    A $^-9$

    B $^-8$

    C   0

    D   9

    E   None of these

15. $3\overline{)41.1} =$

    A   13.7

    B   1.37

    C   137

    D   0.137

    E   None of these

16. $2^3 - 3 =$

A 3

B -1

C 1

D 5

E None of these

17. $5 - {}^-7 =$

A 2

B -2

C 12

D -12

E None of these

18. $\dfrac{2.43}{0.6} =$

A 4.05

B 40.5

C 0.405

D 405

E None of these

19. $3 + 12 \div 2 - 2 =$

A 15

B 5.5

C 7

D 11

E None of these

20. ${}^-9 \times {}^-12 =$

A 98

B ${}^-98$

C 21

D ${}^-21$

E None of these

21.
$$4\frac{3}{8}$$
$$+2\frac{1}{4}$$

A $6\frac{1}{3}$

B $6\frac{7}{8}$

C $7\frac{5}{8}$

D $6\frac{5}{8}$

E None of these

22. $\dfrac{3}{7} \times \dfrac{2}{5} =$

A $\dfrac{5}{12}$

B $\dfrac{6}{35}$

C $\dfrac{29}{35}$

D $\dfrac{1}{2}$

E None of these

23. 20% of 50 =

A 10

B 15

C 20

D 25

E None of these

24. $(5 + {}^-6)^2 + 4$

   A   5

   B   3

   C   −5

   D   65

   E   None of these

25. 10% of __ = 24

   A   2.4

   B   24

   C   240

   D   2400

   E   None of these

26. $-540/-6 =$

   A   −90

   B   9

   C   −9

   D   90

   E   None of these

27. $\frac{18}{7} \div 2 =$

   A $\frac{36}{7}$

   B $\frac{9}{7}$

   C $\frac{16}{7}$

   D   2

   E   None of these

28. $\sqrt{64} + \sqrt{9}$

   A $\sqrt{73}$

   B   36.5

   C   11

   D $\sqrt{55}$

   E   None of these

29. $1\frac{1}{2} \times 2\frac{1}{2} =$

   A $3\frac{3}{4}$

   B   4

   C $2\frac{1}{4}$

   D   3

   E   None of these

30. __ % of \$20.00 = \$12.00

   A   20

   B   40

   C   60

   D   80

   E   None of these

31. $8 - 2^2 + 6 =$

   A   10

   B   42

   C   12

   D   100

   E   None of these

32. $(^-3 - 6) \times {}^-2 =$

A 6

B −6

C ⁻18

D 18

E None of these

33. 120% of 60 =

A 72

B 7.2

C 12

D 80

E None of these

34. 3706 =

A $3 \times 10^3 + 7 \times 10^2 + 6 \times 10$

B $3 \times 10^3 + 7 \times 10^2 + 6$

C $3 \times 10^4 + 7 \times 10^3 + 6 \times 10$

D $3 \times 10^4 + 7 \times 10^2 + 6$

E None of these

35. $6\frac{5}{12} - 3\frac{7}{8} =$

A $3\frac{2}{3}$

B $2\frac{13}{24}$

C $2\frac{1}{2}$

D $3\frac{1}{4}$

E None of these

36. $3(x^2 - 4) =$

A $3x^2 - 4$

B $3x^2 - 7$

C $3x^2 - 12$

D $9x^2 - 24$

E None of these

37. 18% __ = 36

A 6.48

B 20

C 200

D 50

E None of these

38. $2^3 \times 3^2 =$

A 36

B 54

C 48

D 72

E None of these

39. $\dfrac{0.64}{0.008} =$

A 0.8

B 8

C 80

D 800

E None of these

40. $(3^2 - 2^2)^2 =$

A 65

B 25

C 4

D 1

E None of these

PART II. Applied Mathematics
Note: Calculator Permitted

Date: _____   **Start Time:** _____

1. Chris plans to take a 260-mile trip on which he knows he can average 55 miles per hour. To the nearest minute, how long will this trip take?

    A   4 hours

    B   4 hours 12 minutes

    C   4 hours 32 minutes

    D   4 hours 44 minutes

2. If this pattern continues, which of the following figures will be next?

    △ △△△ △△△△△

    A   △△△△△

    B   △△△△△△△

    C   △△△△△△△

    D   △△△△△△△

3. Phil can lower his heating bill by 5% if he sets his thermostat one degree lower than its current setting. If his average monthly bill is $82, how much would he save each month by lowering the thermostat one degree?

    A $4.10

    B $5.00

    C $8.20

    D $10.00

The following table shows the country of origin of 359 autos parked by students and staff at a local university. Use this table to answer questions 4–6.

	Student	Staff	Total
American	107	105	212
European	33	12	45
Asian	55	47	102
Total	195	164	359

4. What percent of all cars surveyed were foreign?

    A   69%

    B   41%

    C   13%

    D   28%

5. What percent of American cars are owned by students?

    A   55%

    B   30%

    C   50%

    D   40%

6. What is the probability that a member of the staff owns a car of Asian origin?

    A   0.45

    B   0.41

    C   0.34

    D   0.29

The following chart shows the monthly sales of high-definition television sets during the past 6 months. Use this chart to answer questions 7 and 8 next.

Month	Number of Sales
January	34
February	26
March	28
April	35
May	42
June	40

7. What was the median number of sales?

A   31.5

B   34.5

C   42

D   26

8. What was the range of the number of sales?

A   6

B   8

C   10

D   16

9. A recipe calls for $\frac{3}{4}$ cup of butter. The low-fat version of this recipe replaces half the butter with an equal amount of margarine. How much margarine should be put in the recipe?

A $\frac{1}{4}$ cup

B $\frac{1}{2}$ cup

C $\frac{2}{3}$ cup

D $\frac{3}{8}$ cup

10. What number is missing from this number pattern?

1   2   4   ____   16   32

A   6

B   8

C   10

D   12

11. What is the geometric name for the shape of a stop sign, shown next.

A   Trapezoid

B   Hexagon

C   Octagon

D   Decagon

Following is a portion of Suzanne's checkbook register. Based on this information, answer questions 12–15.

Date	Check#	Description	Withdrawal	Deposit	Balance
5/31					$1480.45
6/1	567	rent	$650		
6/1	568	car payment	$250		
6/3		paycheck		$1280.64	
6/3	569	grocery store	$92.53		
6/5	570	cable	$45.20		
6/8		ATM	$100		

12. Suzanne will be getting a 5% raise with her next paycheck. Which expression shows how to find the amount of her next paycheck?

A $1280.64 × 10.0

B $1280.64 × 1.10

C $1280.64 × 1.05

D $1280.64 × 0.10

13. Suzanne's cable bill will not change for at least a year. How much will she pay for cable service in 1 year?

A $452.00

B $542.40

C $642.50

D $684.40

14. What is the difference between Suzanne's balance on 5/31 and 6/8?

A   Increase of $143.11

B   Increase of $1623.36

C   Decrease of $109.72

D   Increase of $142.91

15. Suzanne's friend will be staying with her through the summer and has agreed to split the rent and cable for the three months she's there. How much money will she pay Suzanne for the three months?

A   About $900

B   About $1000

C   About $1200

D   About $1500

16. The following bar chart shows the number of oil spills resulting from each cause. Which cause led to the spill of the most oil?

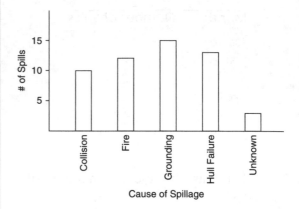

A   Collision

B   Fire

C   Hull failure

D   Cannot be determined

17. The sign on a club states, "You must be at least 21 to enter." If *x* represents your age, which of the following is the mathematical way of saying this?

A $x > 21$

B $x \geq 21$

C $x < 21$

D $x \leq 21$

18. Forty percent of the employees at Apple Aerospace are female. Of these, 25% have blonde hair. If the company has 500 employees, how many blonde females work at Apple Aerospace?

A   50

B   325

C   125

D   200

19. The volume of a sphere is given by the formula $V = \frac{4}{3}\pi r^3$, where $\pi \approx 3.14$ and r is the radius of the sphere. What is the approximate volume of the following sphere?

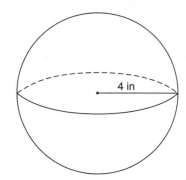

4 in

A   268 cubic inches

B   101 cubic inches

C   58 cubic inches

D   34 cubic inches

20. A 20-man golf league paid $15 per man for dinner following its year-end tournament. Each man left $3 toward a tip for the waitstaff. What percent tip did the group leave?

A   12%

B   15%

C   18%

D   20%

The following graph shows figures on a coordinate grid. Problems 21–23 are based on this graph.

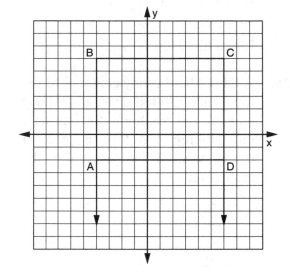

21. What are the coordinates of point B?

A   (4,6)

B   (⁻4,6)

C   (4,⁻6)

D   (⁻4,⁻6)

22. Which segment lies on a ray?

A $\overline{AB}$

B $\overline{BC}$

C $\overline{AD}$

D   All 3 of these lie on rays.

23. What is the length of segment $\overline{CD}$?

A   2

B   6

C   8

D   10

24. Simplify the expression $8x + 3y - 5x$.

    A $3x + 3y$

    B $13x + 3y$

    C $6xy$

    D $11xy - 5x$

25. A bag of hard candy contains 12 yellow candies, 8 red ones, and 9 green ones. If you reach into the bag without looking and take a piece of candy, what is the probability that it's not red?

    A $\dfrac{8}{21}$

    B $\dfrac{8}{12}$

    C $\dfrac{21}{29}$

    D $\dfrac{8}{29}$

26. Jim walks 5 feet north and 12 feet west. How far is he from his starting point?

    A   17 feet

    B   14.5 feet

    C   13 feet

    D   12 feet

27. Which of the following equations represents the statement, "Five less than three times a number is more than ten."

    A $5 - 3x > 10$

    B $3x - 5 > 10$

    C $3x - 5 \geq 10$

    D $5 - 3x \geq 10$

The diagram shows a circle with center C and several points labeled on the circle. Use this figure to answer problems 28 and 29.

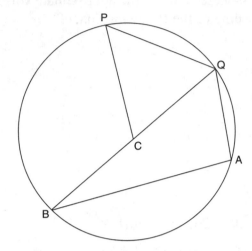

28. Which of these is a radius of the circle?

    A $\overline{PQ}$

    B $\overline{PC}$

    C $\overline{AB}$

    D $\overline{QA}$

29. If the length of $\overline{BC}$ is 5 centimeters, what is the circumference of the circle? ($C = \pi d$)

    A 2π centimeters

    B 5π centimeters

    C 7π centimeters

    D 10π centimeters

The following graph shows the weekly average price of two brands of gasoline. Prices are rounded up to the nearest whole cent. Use this graph to answer questions 30–33.

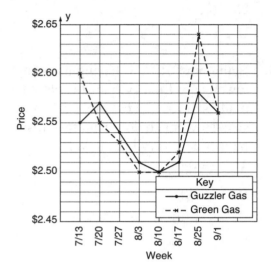

30. What was the price of Guzzler gasoline on 7/27?

 A $2.54

 B $2.63

 C $2.55

 D $2.51

31. For how many weeks was Green Gas cheaper than Guzzler Gas?

 A 1

 B 2

 C 3

 D 4

32. In how many weeks did the price of Guzzler gas increase while the price of Green gas decreased?

 A 1

 B 2

 C 3

 D 4

33. During how many weeks were the prices of Guzzler Gas and Green Gas the same?

 A 1

 B 2

 C 3

 D 4

34. What values of x will make the inequality true?

$3x - 4 < 5$

 A $x < 3$

 B $x < 4$

 C $x < \dfrac{1}{3}$

 D $x < 7$

35. What is the next number in this number sequence?

10   7   3 $^-2$ $^-8$ —

 A $^-14$

 B $^-15$

 C $^-16$

 D $^-17$

36. Suppose the diameter of a certain atom is 0.00000026 cm. In scientific notation, this would be written as

 A 26×10^{-7}

 B 2.6×10^{-7}

 C 2.6×10^{8}

 D 2.6×10^{-8}

The graph shows figures on a coordinate grid. Use this graph to do problems 37–40.

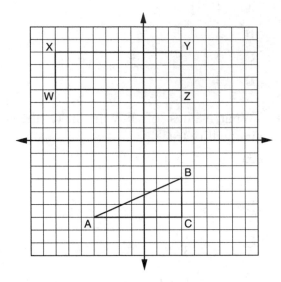

37. What is the area of $\triangle ABC$?

    A   10 square units

    B   10.5 square units

    C   17 square units

    D   21 square units

38. What is the perimeter of rectangle *XYWZ*?

    A   30 units

    B   26 units

    C   15 units

    D   13 units

39. If the triangle were translated 2 units up and 7 units left, what would be the new location of point *B*?

    A   (2, 7)

    B   (2, ⁻7)

    C   (⁻4, ⁻1)

    D   (⁻4, 1)

40. Which of the following points lies inside the triangle?

    A   (⁻3, ⁻5)

    B   (3, ⁻6)

    C   (0, ⁻5)

    D   (⁻5, 0)

41. Bathrooms 'R Us is having its annual towel sale. Luxury bath towels normally sell for $14 but are 20% off on sale. How much does Rita save if she buys four luxury bath towels?

    A $2.80

    B $8.00

    C $11.20

    D $16.00

42. Todd plans to carpet his L-shaped family room, shown in the following diagram. Allowing 15% waste, how many square feet of carpeting does Todd have to buy in order to carpet this room?

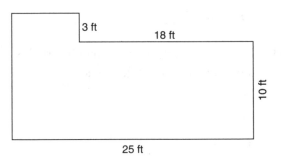

    A   275 square feet

    B   300 square feet

    C   312 square feet

    D   340 square feet

43. A dinner party of 20 consists of 12 females, 8 teenagers, and 5 teenage females. How many at the party are males who are not teenagers?

A   9

B   7

C   5

D   3

44. What is the volume of the box shown?

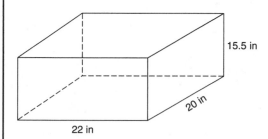

15.5 in

20 in

22 in

A   57.5 cubic inches

B   834 cubic inches

C   3300 cubic inches

D   6820 cubic inches

45. What value of x makes the equation true?

$\frac{2}{3}x + 4 = 12$

A $x = 8$

B $x = 9$

C $x = 12$

D $x = 24$

46. Which of the following is closest to 5.67 hours?

A   5 hours, 35 minutes

B   5 hours, 40 minutes

C   5 hours, 45 minutes

D   5 hours, 50 minutes

47. The directions on a paint can say that you can thin the paint by adding a $\frac{1}{2}$ pint of water per gallon of paint. How many quarts of water need to be added to thin a 10-gallon drum of paint?

A   1 quart

B $1\frac{1}{4}$ quarts

C $1\frac{1}{2}$ quarts

D   2 quarts

48. Cooking instructions call for $\frac{1}{4}$ teaspoon of salt for 2 servings. How many teaspoons of salt should be used for 7 servings?

A $1\frac{1}{2}$ teaspoons

B $1\frac{1}{7}$ teaspoons

C $\frac{7}{8}$ teaspoon

D $\frac{2}{3}$ teaspoon

49. Which of the following describes the sides of a right triangle?

A   5 units, 8 units, 13 units

B   2 units, 5 units, 6 units

C   7 units, 8 units, 15 units

D   8 units, 15 units 17 units

50. Which equation is equivalent to the following equation?

$2x + 5y = 10$

A $\quad y = \frac{2}{5}x + 2$

B $\quad y = \frac{2}{5}x - 2$

C $\quad y = \frac{-2}{5}x + 2$

D $\quad y = \frac{-2}{5}x - 2$

Pretest Answer Key, Lesson Key, and Problem Type
Part I: Mathematics Computation

Question	Answer	Lesson	Problem Type
1	D	1	Subtracting decimals
2	A	3	Dividing integers
3	A	2	Adding mixed numbers
4	C	6	Solving equations
5	A	4	Finding the part in a percent problem
6	D	5	Evaluating a square root
7	B	3	Adding integers
8	B	1	Subtracting decimals
9	A	2	Subtracting mixed numbers
10	B	5	Evaluating numerical expressions
11	C	1	Adding decimals
12	B	3	Adding integers
13	D	1	Scientific notation
14	A	3	Subtracting integers
15	A	1	Dividing decimals
16	D	5	Evaluating numerical expressions
17	C	3	Subtracting integers
18	A	1	Dividing decimals
19	C	5	Evaluating numerical expressions
20	E	3	Multiplying integers
21	D	2	Adding mixed numbers
22	B	2	Multiplying fractions
23	A	4	Finding the part in a percent problem
24	A	5	Evaluating numerical expressions
25	C	4	Finding the whole in a percent problem
26	D	3	Dividing integers
27	B	2	Dividing fractions
28	C	5	Evaluating square roots
29	A	2	Multiplying mixed numbers
30	C	4	Finding % in a percent problem
31	A	5	Evaluating numerical expressions
32	D	3	Subtracting and multiplying integers
33	A	4	Finding the part in a percent problem
34	B	1	Writing decimal numbers
35	B	2	Subtracting mixed numbers
36	C	6	Simplifying expressions
37	C	4	Finding the whole in percent problem
38	D	5	Evaluating numerical expressions
39	C	1	Dividing decimals
40	B	5	Evaluating numerical expressions

Part II: Applied Mathematics

Question	Answer	Lesson	Problem Type
1	D	7	Story problem on travel
2	B	8	Picture pattern
3	A	7	Story problem on %
4	B	12	Counting cases and %
5	C	12	Counting cases and %
6	D	12	Counting cases and proportion
7	B	12	Probability/Statistics
8	D	12	Probability/Statistics
9	D	7	Multiplying fractions
10	B	8	Number sequences
11	C	9	Geometry Definitions
12	C	12	Data interpretation
13	B	12	Data interpretation
14	D	12	Data interpretation
15	B	7	Story problem
16	D	12	Data interpretation
17	B	8	Words to symbols
18	A	7	Story problem on %
19	A	9	Volume
20	D	7	Story problem on %
21	B	11	Coordinates of a point
22	A	9	Geometry Definitions
23	C	11	Coordinate geometry
24	A	6	Simplifying expressions
25	C	12	Probability
26	C	9	Triangles—Pythagorean Theorem
27	B	8	Words to symbols
28	B	9	Geometry Definitions
29	D	9	Perimeter
30	A	12	Data interpretation
31	C	12	Data interpretation
32	A	12	Data interpretation
33	B	12	Data interpretation
34	A	6	Solving inequalities
35	B	8	Number sequences
36	B	7	Story problem on scientific notation
37	B	9	Area
38	B	9	Perimeter
39	C	11	Coordinate geometry
40	C	11	Coordinate geometry
41	C	7	Story problem on %

Question	Answer	Lesson	Problem Type
42	C	9	Area and %
43	C	12	Counting using a Venn diagram
44	D	9	Volume
45	C	6	Solving equations
46	B	10	Time measurement
47	B	10	Units of liquid volume
48	C	7	Story problem—fractions
49	D	9	Triangles—Pythagorean Theorem
50	C	6	Equivalent equations

Pretest Answer Explanations
Mathematics Computation

1.	D	3.17	Line up the decimal points and subtract.
2.	A	−5	Dividing numbers with different signs makes the answer negative.
3.	A	10	First change the mixed numbers to improper fractions.

$6\frac{7}{8} + 3\frac{1}{8} = \frac{55}{8} + \frac{25}{8}$. Since the fractions have the same denominator, add the numerators: $\frac{55}{8} + \frac{25}{8} = \frac{80}{8}$. $\frac{80}{8}$ means $80 \div 8 = 10$.

4.	C	4	Subtract 3 from both sides of the equation: $x + 3 - 3 = 7 - 3$. The result is $x = 4$.
5.	A	50	You are looking for the part in a percent problem.

$$Part = \% \times Whole \div 100 = 10 \times 500 \div 100 = 50$$

6.	D	10	$\sqrt{100} = 10$ because $10^2 = 10 \times 10 = 100$.
7.	B	$^-7$	When adding numbers with different signs, ignore the signs and subtract the smaller number from the larger one. The answer has the sign of the larger number.
8.	B	0.113	Line up the decimal points, write 0.22 as 0.220, and subtract.
9.	A	$3\frac{1}{6}$	First change the mixed numbers to improper fractions:

$6\frac{1}{2} - 3\frac{1}{3} = \frac{13}{2} - \frac{10}{3}$. Since the denominators are different, you need a common denominator. The smallest number that both 2 and 3 divide evenly into is 6, so 6 is the least common denominator. Change each number so its denominator is 6: $\frac{13}{2} = \frac{13 \times 3}{2 \times 3} = \frac{39}{6}$ and $\frac{10}{3} = \frac{10 \times 2}{3 \times 2} = \frac{20}{6}$. Then subtract $\frac{39}{6} - \frac{20}{6} = \frac{19}{6}$. Change $\frac{19}{6}$ to a mixed number by dividing, to get $3\frac{1}{6}$.

10.	B	13	$2^2 + 3^2 = (2 \times 2) + (3 \times 3) = 4 + 9 = 13$.
11.	C	38.721	Line up the decimal points, write 38.4 as 38.400, and add.
12.	B	$^-1$	First add 7 and $^-5$ to get 2. (Ignore the signs, subtract the smaller number from the larger one, and give the answer the sign of the larger one.) Then add 2 and $^-3$ to get $^-1$. (Same rule.)
13.	D	0.0027	The exponent $^-3$ tells you that the answer will be smaller than 1. Therefore, move the decimal point three places to the left.
14.	A	$^-9$	$0 - 9 = 0 + {}^-9 = {}^-9$.
15.	A	13.7	Do the division, and place the decimal point above the one in the dividend.
16.	D	5	$2^3 - 3 = (2 \times 2 \times 2) - 3 = 8 - 3 = 5$.

17. C 12 — Subtract means add the opposite, and the opposite of $^-7$ is 7, so $5 - {}^-7 = 5 + 7 = 12$.

18. A 4.05 — Multiply both numerator and denominator by 10. This doesn't change the fraction because $\frac{10}{10} = 1$: $\frac{2.43}{0.6} = \frac{2.43 \times 10}{0.6 \times 10} = \frac{24.3}{6}$. Do the division, and place the decimal above the decimal in the dividend.

19. C 7 — Follow the order of operations, and do the division first: $12 \div 2 = 6$. Then add $3 + 6$ to get 9, and subtract 2 to get 7.

20. E — When you multiply two numbers together that have the same sign, the answer is positive. $^-9 \times {}^-12 = 108$, so the answer is "None of these."

21. D $6\frac{5}{8}$ — First change the numbers to improper fractions: $4\frac{3}{8} + 2\frac{1}{4} = \frac{35}{8} + \frac{9}{4}$. Since the denominators are different, you need a common denominator. The smallest number that both 8 and 4 divide into evenly is 8, so 8 is the least common denominator. The denominator of $\frac{35}{8}$ is already 8, so nothing has to be done to this number. To change the denominator of $\frac{9}{4}$ to 8, multiply both numerator and denominator by 2: $\frac{9}{4} = \frac{18}{8}$. Now add: $\frac{35}{8} + \frac{18}{8} = \frac{53}{8}$. Change $\frac{53}{8}$ by dividing, to get the mixed number $6\frac{5}{8}$.

22. B $\frac{6}{35}$ — Multiply the numerators and multiply the denominators, to get $\frac{3}{7} \times \frac{2}{5} = \frac{6}{35}$.

23. A 10 — You are looking for the part in a percent problem.
$Part = \% \times Whole \div 100 = 20 \times 50 \div 100 = 10$

24. A 5 — Following the order of operations, do the addition in the parentheses first: $5 + {}^-6 = {}^-1$. Then raise $^-1$ to the second power: $^-1 \times {}^-1 = 1$. Then add $1 + 4 = 5$.

25. C 240 — You are looking for the whole in a percent problem.
$Whole = Part \div \% \times 100 = 24 \div 10 \times 100 = 240$

26. D 90 — When you divide two numbers with the same sign, the answer is positive, so $^-540 \div {}^-6 = 90$.

27. B $\frac{9}{7}$ — The number 2 is the same as the fraction $\frac{2}{1}$. To divide by $\frac{2}{1}$, multiply by $\frac{1}{2}$. So $\frac{18}{7} \div 2 = \frac{\cancel{18}^9}{7} \times \frac{1}{\cancel{2}_1} = \frac{9 \times 1}{7 \times 1} = \frac{9}{7}$.

28. C 11 — $\sqrt{64} = 8$ and $\sqrt{9} = 3$, and $8 + 3 = 11$.

29. A $3\frac{3}{4}$

First change the mixed numbers to fractions: $1\frac{1}{2} = \frac{3}{2}$ and $2\frac{1}{2} = \frac{5}{2}$. Then multiply the fractions by multiplying numerators and denominators: $\frac{3}{2} \times \frac{5}{2} = \frac{15}{4}$. Change $\frac{15}{4}$ to the mixed number $3\frac{3}{4}$.

30. C 60

You are looking for the % in a percent problem.
$\% = Part \div Whole \times 100 = 12 \div 20 \times 100 = 60$

31. A 10

Following the order of operations, do $2^2 = 4$ first. Then $8 - 4 + 6 = 10$.

32. D 18

Following the order of operations, first do $^-3 - 6$. Subtract means add the opposite, so $^-3 - 6 = ^-3 + ^-6$. When you add two numbers with the same sign, add the numbers ignoring the sign, and attach the sign to the answer: $^-3 + ^-6 = ^-9$. Then multiply this answer by $^-2$: $^-9 \times ^-2 = 18$. The answer is positive because the two factors have the same sign.

33. A 72

You are looking for the part in a percent problem.
$Part = \% \times Whole \div 100 = 120 \div 60 \div 100 = 72$

34. B $3 \times 10^3 + 7 \times 10^2 + 6$

$3706 = 3000 + 700 + 6 = (3 \times 1000) + (7 \times 100) + 6$
$= 3 \times 10^3 + 7 \times 10^2 + 6$

35. B $2\frac{13}{24}$

First change the mixed numbers to improper fractions: $6\frac{5}{12} - 3\frac{7}{8} = \frac{77}{12} - \frac{31}{8}$. Since the denominators are different, you need a common denominator. The smallest number that both 12 and 8 divide into is 24, so 24 is the least common denominator. Change each fraction so the denominator is 24: $\frac{77}{12} = \frac{77 \times 2}{12 \times 2} = \frac{154}{24}$ and $\frac{31}{8} = \frac{31 \times 3}{8 \times 3} = \frac{93}{24}$. Subtract the numerators to get $\frac{154}{24} - \frac{93}{24} = \frac{61}{24}$. Change $\frac{61}{24}$ to the mixed number $2\frac{13}{24}$.

36. C $3x^2 - 12$

Use the Distributive Property: $3(x^2 - 4) = 3x^2 - 3(4) = 3x^2 - 12$.

37. C 200

You are looking for the whole in a percent problem.
$Whole = Part \div \% \times 100 = 36 \div 18 \times 100 = 200$

38. D 72

$2^3 \times 3^2 = (2 \times 2 \times 2) \times (3 \times 3) = 8 \times 9 = 72$

39. C 80

Multiply numerator and denominator by 1000 by moving each decimal point three places to the right. You need to add a 0 to the number in the numerator: $\frac{.64}{.008} = \frac{640}{8}$. Then divide to get 80.

40. B 25

Following the order of operations, do what's in the parentheses first. Do exponents before subtraction, so $3^2 - 2^2 = 9 - 4 = 5$. Now square what's in the parentheses: $(3^2 - 2^2)^2 = 5^2 = 25$.

Applied Mathematics

1. D 4 hours 44 minutes

Use the formula *time = dist ÷ speed* to get *time* = 260 ÷ 55 = 4.73 hours. Multiply .73 × 60 = 43.8 ≈ 44 minutes.

2. B ▲△▲△▲△

The pattern begins with a dark triangle and then alternates between dark and light triangles. Each step in the pattern adds two more triangles.

3. A $4.10

You are looking for the part in a percent problem. The whole is 82 and the % is 5.

$$Part = \% \times Whole \div 100 = 5 \times 82 \div 100 = 4.1$$

4. B 41%

You are looking for the % in a percent problem. The whole is 359, and the part is 45 + 102 = 147 (European + Asian).

$$\% = Part \div Whole \times 100 = 147 \div 359 \times 100 = 41.$$

5. C 50%

You are looking for the % in a percent problem. The whole is the total number of American cars (212), and the part is the number of students who own American cars (107).

$$\% = Part \div Whole \times 100 = 107 \div 212 \times 100 = 50.$$

6. D .29

The probability that a staff member owns an Asian car is similar to a percent problem, except the answer is expressed as a decimal instead of a percent.

In this case, the probability is $\frac{47}{164}$ = 0.29.

7. B 34.5

If there is an even number of numbers in order from smallest to largest, the median is the average of the two middle numbers. In this problem, there are 6 numbers, so the median is the average of the 3rd and 4th numbers in the ordered list (34 + 35) ÷ 2 = 34.5.

8. D 16

The range is the largest number minus the smallest number: 42 − 26 = 16.

9. D $\frac{3}{8}$

The problem asks you to find one-half of $\frac{3}{4}$. In math, the word "of" means times. Calculate $\frac{1}{2} \times \frac{3}{4} = \frac{3}{8}$.

10. B 8

Each number in the sequence is two times the number before it. The number before the blank is 4, and 2 × 4 = 8.

11. C Octagon

The stop sign has eight sides. This is an octagon.

12. C $1280.64 × 1.05

You can use a shortcut for this problem. Her next paycheck will consist of the original 1 × $1280.64 *plus* 0.05 × $1280.64, or (1 + 0.05) × $1280.64.

13. B $542.40 Multiply Suzanne's monthly cable bill by 12:
$45.20 × 12 = $542.40.

14. D increase of $142.91. Subtract the 5 withdrawals from the deposit:
1280.64 − 650 − 250 − 92.53 − 45.20 − 100 = 142.91

15. B About $1000. Monthly rent and cable amounts, sum to $695.20, so 3 months would be $2085.60. Divide this by 2 to get $1042.80. The closest answer choice is B. About $1000.

16. D Cannot be determined. The highest bar is the "Grounding" category, but this is tops in the number of spills, not the amount of oil spilled. The bar chart doesn't provide information on the amount of oil spilled.

17. B $x \geq 21$ "At least" means "Greater than or equal to."

18. A 50 You are looking for the part (twice) in a percent problem. First, with a whole of 500 and a % of 40, find the number of women: 40 ÷ 500 × 100 = 200. Of the 200 women (the new whole) and a % of 25, find the number of blonde women: 200 × 25 ÷ 100 = 50.

19. A 268 cubic inches Substitute 4 into the formula: $V = \frac{4}{3} \times \pi \times 4^3 \approx 268$, or
$$V = \frac{4}{3} \times 3.14 \times 4 \times 4 \times 4 \approx 268$$

20. D 20% You are looking for the % in a percent problem. Because each man left the same amount for the dinner and the same tip, you can calculate the percent for each man, and this will be the same percent for the whole dinner:
% = Part ÷ Whole × 100 = 3 ÷ 15 × 100 = 20
You would get the same answer if the part and the whole were each 20 times these amounts.

21. B (−4, 6) To get to the point from the origin (0,0), you have to go 4 to the left (x negative) and 6 up (y positive).

22. A $\overline{AB}$ A ray extends forever in one direction. This is indicated by the arrowhead. $\overline{CD}$ also lies on a ray, but this isn't an answer choice.

23. C 8 There are eight spaces from point C to point D.

24. A $3x + 3y$ 8x and 5x are like terms, and subtraction is indicated: 8x − 5x = 3x.

25. C $\frac{21}{29}$ There are 12 + 8 + 9 = 29 pieces of candy altogether, and 12 + 9 = 21 are not red. Therefore the probability is $\frac{21}{29}$.

26. C   13 feet

When you walk west after walking north, you are turning at a right angle. (See the following figure.) The two paths of the walk and the direct line path form a right triangle with leg lengths 5 feet and 12 feet. Use the Pythagorean Theorem to get $c^2 = 5^2 + 12^2 = 25 + 144 = 169$. Then $c = \sqrt{169} = 13$.

27. B $3x - 5 > 10$

"Three times a number" can be represented by $3x$, and 5 less than that is $3x - 5$. Therefore, $3x - 5 > 10$ is the correct mathematical statement.

28. B $\overline{PC}$

A radius is a segment from a circle to its center.

29. D 10π centimeters

$\overline{BC}$ is a radius with length 5. The diameter of the circle is twice the radius, so the diameter d is 10. Use the formula given in the problem to get $D = 10\pi$ centimeters.

30. A $2.54

Each grid line on the vertical axis stands for one cent. The point for Guzzler Gas on 7/27 is one grid line below $2.55.

31. C   3

Points on the dashed line (Green Gas) are below points on the solid line (Guzzler Gas) on 7/20, 7/27, and 8/3. Green Gas was cheaper for 3 weeks.

32. A   1

There is only one place on the graph where the solid line is going up (from left to right) while the dashed line is going down: between 7/13 and 7/20.

33. B   2

The prices were the same on 8/10 and 9/1.

34. A $x < 3$

To solve the inequality, add 4 to both sides:

$3x - 4 + 4 < 5 + 4$. This results in the inequality $3x < 9$. Then divide both sides by 3: $\frac{3x}{3} < \frac{9}{3}$. This results in the inequality $x < 3$.

35. B $^-15$

The numbers are going down, first by 3, then by 4, and so forth. Each time the next number goes down one more than the previous time. Since it goes down by 6 to get from $^-2$ to $^-8$, it goes down by 7 to get to the next number, $^-15$.

36. B 2.6×10^{-7} You have to move the decimal point 7 spaces to change the given number to a number between 1 and 10 (2.6). Since the original number is less than 1, the exponent is negative.

37. B   10.5 square units   The length of $\overline{AB}$ is 7, and the length of $\overline{BC}$ is 3. Since $\triangle ABC$ is a right triangle, these lengths are the base and altitude of the triangle. The area is

$$\frac{1}{2}bh = \frac{1}{2}(7)(3) = 10.5.$$

38. B   26 units   Perimeter is the distance around. The length of $\overline{XY}$ is 10, and the length of $\overline{YZ}$ is 3. The perimeter is $2 \times 10 + 2 \times 3 = 26$.

39. C   ($^-$4, $^-$1)   Point B is at (3, $^-$3). Up means add 2 to the y-coordinate: $^-$3 + 2 = $^-$1 and left means subtract 7 from the x-coordinate: 3 − 7 = 3 + $^-$7 = $^-$4.

40. C   (0, $^-$5)   Test the points one at a time, remembering that the first coordinate tells you to move right (+) or left (−), and the second one tells you to move up (+) or down (−).

41. C $11.20   You are looking for the part in a percent problem. The whole is 14, and % is 20. *Part = % × Whole ÷* 100 = 20 × 14 ÷ 100 = 2.8. You save $2.80 on each towel, so you save 4 × $2.80 = $11.20 on 4 towels.

42. C   312 square feet   First you need to find the area of the floor. Divide the room as shown in the figure following.

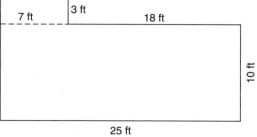

Since the length of one side of the room is 25 feet, and the length of the opposite side to the L is 18, the length of the dashed segment is 25 − 18 = 7. The dashed segment gives you a 7 by 3-foot rectangle and a 25 by 10-foot rectangle. The total area is 7 × 3 + 25 × 10 = 271 square feet. Allowing for 15% waste, you have to buy 1.15 times 271, which rounds to 312 square feet.

43. C   5

Use a Venn diagram to solve this. (See following figure.) The rectangle

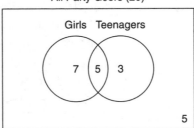

All Party-Goers (20)

represents the whole party of 20. One circle represents girls and the other circle represents teenagers. The overlap of the two circles represents teenage girls. Start by putting 5 in this overlap. Since there are 12 girls, put 7 in the part of the Girls circle that does not overlap. Since there are 8 teenagers, put 3 in the part of the Teenagers circle that does not overlap. Now add all three numbers in the circles: 7 + 5 + 3 = 15. The rest of the people at the party (20 − 15 = 5) are neither girls nor teenagers—in other words, boys who are not teenagers.

44. D   6820 cubic inches

To get the volume of a box, multiply the three measurements:
$$22 \times 20 \times 15.5 = 6820.$$

45. C   12

First subtract 4 from both sides: $\frac{2}{3}x + 4 - 4 = 12 - 4$. The result it $\frac{2}{3}x = 8$.

Then multiply both sides by the reciprocal $\frac{3}{2}$ of $\frac{2}{3}$:
$\frac{3}{2}\left(\frac{2}{3}x\right) = \frac{3}{2}(8)$. The result is $x = 12$.

46. B   5 hours, 40 minutes.

Multiply 0.67 hours by 60 minutes per hour to get 40.2 minutes.

47. B $1\frac{1}{4}$ quarts

You need to add ten $\frac{1}{2}$ pints of water to a 10-gallon drum. This is 5 pints of water. There are 4 pints to a quart, so 5 pints is $\frac{5}{4} = 1\frac{1}{4}$ quarts.

48. C $\frac{7}{8}$ teaspoon

Since 7 servings is $3\frac{1}{2}$ times 2 servings, you need $3\frac{1}{2}$ times as much salt:
$$3\frac{1}{2} \times \frac{1}{4} = \frac{7}{2} \times \frac{1}{4} = \frac{7}{8}.$$

49. D   8 units, 15, units, 17 units

You have to determine which answer choice fits the formula $a^2 + b^2 = c^2$, where a and b are the two smaller numbers. Only answer choice D works: $8^2 + 15^2 = 64 + 225 = 289 = 17^2$.

50. C $y = \dfrac{-2}{5}x + 2$

You have to solve this equation for y (get y by itself on one side of the equation). First subtract $2x$ from both sides: $-2x + 2x + 5y = 10 - 2x$. The result is $5y = 10 - 2x$. Now divide both sides of the equation by 5:

$$\frac{5y}{5} = \frac{10 - 2x}{5} = 2 + \frac{-2}{5}x = \frac{-2}{5}x + 2.$$

DECIMALS

Our number system uses a base of 10. This means that most numbers you will ever encounter can be written as a decimal. *Deci* is the Latin prefix that means 10. While most people think of decimal numbers as being less than 1, numbers larger than 1 are also decimals. The most familiar use of decimal numbers is writing amounts of money—dollars and cents. To explain the meaning of base 10 numbers, or decimals, we need to review exponents.

- Numbers larger than 1 are also decimals.

An **exponent** is a count of the number of times a **base** number multiplies itself. It is written "in the air" (a superscript) to the right of the base. For example, 10^3 means $10 \times 10 \times 10$. The small superscript *3* means the base number 10 is multiplied 3 times, so $10^3 = 1000$.

- A common mistake is to use the exponent as a multiplier; but $2^3 = 8$, not 6.

When the base number is 10, the exponent is also the number of zeros following the 1 in 10. Thus $10^0 = 1$ (no zeros), $10^1 = 10$ (1 zero), $10^2 = 100$ (2 zeros), $10^3 = 1000$ (3 zeros), $10^4 = 10,000$ (4 zeros), and so forth.

This pattern continues in the opposite direction, but now the exponents are negative numbers. This time the exponent, without the negative sign, counts how far to the *right* of the decimal point to place the 1. Thus $10^{-1} = 0.1$ (1st place to the right of the decimal point), $10^{-2} = 0.01$ (2nd place to the right of the decimal point), $10^{-3} = 0.001$ (3rd place to the right of the decimal point), $10^{-4} = 0.0001$ (4th place to the right of the decimal), and so forth.

- Positive powers of 10 are larger than 1; negative powers of 10 are smaller than 1; and $10^0 = 1$.

Powers of 10 are called *place values*. You learned the names of these place values in elementary school. The **units** place value corresponds to 10^0; the **tens** place value corresponds to 10^1; the **hundreds** place value corresponds to 10^2; and so forth. In the other direction, the **tenths** place value corresponds to 10^{-1}; the **hundredths** place value corresponds to 10^{-2}; and so forth. Powers of 10 and their place value names are summarized in the following table.

Place Values

Whole Numbers												Decimals				
Billions			Millions			Thousands			Units							
10^{11}	10^{10}	10^9	10^8	10^7	10^6	10^5	10^4	10^3	10^2	10^1	10^0	10^{-1}	10^{-2}	10^{-3}	10^{-4}	10^{-5}
Hundred Billions	Ten Billions	Billions	Hundred Millions	Ten Millions	Millions	Hundred Thousands	Ten Thousands	Thousands	Hundreds	Tens	Units	Tenths	Hundredths	Thousandths	Ten Thousandths	Hundred Thousandths

Writing Decimal Numbers

Now we can see how decimal numbers are written. Take, for example, the number 7352—seven thousand three hundred fifty-two. It equals 7 thousands, 3 hundreds, 5 tens, and 2 units. So $7352 = \underline{7} \times 10^3 + \underline{3} \times 10^2 + \underline{5} \times 10^1 + \underline{2} \times 10^0$. In another example, 0.345 is $\underline{3} \times 1 + \underline{4} \times .01 + \underline{5} \times .001$. Using exponents, this is $\underline{3} \times 10^{-1} + \underline{4} \times 10^{-2} + \underline{5} \times 10^{-3}$. One more example is the number 37.042. Using exponents, this is written as $\underline{3} \times 10^1 + \underline{7} \times 10^0 + \underline{0} \times 10^{-1} + \underline{4} \times 10^{-2} + \underline{2} \times 10^{-3}$. Since $0 \times 10^{-1} = 0$, it's not necessary to write that term, so you could also write 37.042 as $\underline{3} \times 10^1 + \underline{7} \times 10^0 + \underline{4} \times 10^{-2} + \underline{2} \times 10^{-3}$.

The decimal number system makes it easy to multiply a number by a power of 10. If you're multiplying a number by a positive power of 10, simply move the decimal point that many places to the right (making the result bigger). For example, to multiply 453.7 by 100, the two zeros in 100 tell you to move the decimal point two places to the right. You can always attach zeros to the end of a number right of the decimal point. In this case, you attach a 0 to write 453.7 as 453.70. Then move the decimal point two places to the right, getting 45,370. If multiplying by a negative power of 10, move the decimal point that many places to the left (making the result smaller). If you multiply 453.7 by .01, move the decimal point two places to the left, getting 4.537.

To divide numbers by powers of 10, do the reverse: if the power of 10 is positive, division makes the result smaller, so move the decimal point to the left; while if the power of 10 is negative, division will make the result larger, so move the decimal point to the right.

- To multiply by powers of 10, move the decimal point to the right if the power is positive.
- To divide by powers of 10, move the decimal point to the left if the power is positive.

Practice Writing Decimals

Write each number using powers of 10.

1. 37   2. 75,021   3. 0.896

4. 1.362   5. 456.301   6. 7000

Write each as a decimal number.

7. $4 \times 10^2 + 8 \times 10^1 + 3$

8. $2 \times 10^4 + 6 \times 10^2 + 5 \times 10^{-1} + 8 \times 10^{-2}$

9. $4 \times 10^6 + 7 \times 10^4 + 3 + 4 \times 10^{-1}$

10. $8 + 1 \times 10^{-1}$

Scientific Notation

Any number can be written in *scientific notation,* but this method is useful for writing very large numbers and numbers that are very close to zero. A number is in scientific notation if it is a number between 1 and 10, times a power of 10. Some examples will illustrate this.

Example A.   Write 35,756 in scientific notation.

As it stands, the decimal point comes after the last digit, so the number is 35,756. To change this to a number between 1 and 10, you need to move the decimal four places to the left—in other words, divide by 10^4. Now you have 3.5756. To return to the original number, you multiply by 10^4, so the scientific notation for 35,756 is 3.5756×10^4.

Example B.   Write .0000439 in scientific notation.

To change this to a number between 1 and 10, you need to move the decimal five places to the right—in other words, multiply by 10^5. Now you have 4.39. To return to the original number, you have to divide by 10^5 or equivalently multiply by 10^{-5}, so the scientific notation for .0000439 is 4.39×10^{-5}.

Putting these two examples together gives a rule for changing from decimal form to scientific notation:

- To write a number in scientific notation, move the decimal point the number of places that results in a number between 1 and 10. Call this number *n.* If the original number is larger than 10, multiply by 10^n to get the scientific notation. If the original number is smaller than 10, multiply by 10^{-n}.

Reversing the process means determining the decimal form of a number in scientific notation.

Example C. Write the number 6.45×10^3 in decimal notation.

When you multiply a number by 10^3, move the decimal point three places to the right (getting a larger number). This gives you the answer 6450.

Example D. Write the number 9.351×10^{-4} in decimal notation.

When you multiply a number by 10^{-4}, move the decimal point four places to the left (getting a smaller number). This gives you the answer 0.0009351.

When numbers are written in scientific notation, it is easy to compare their orders of magnitude. The difference in **order of magnitude** between two numbers is the difference in the exponents when those numbers are written in powers of 10. For example, 105 and 1075 differ by one order of magnitude because $105 = 1.05 \times 10^2$ while $1075 = 1.075 \times 10^3$. The difference in exponents is $3 - 2 = 1$.

The power of an earthquake is measured on the Richter scale. Richter scale numbers represent orders of magnitude. Thus an earthquake of Richter number 8 is a hundred (10^2) times more powerful than an earthquake of Richter number 6.

Practice Scientific Notation

In problems 1–4 change the decimal number to scientific notation.

1. 3,100,000   2. 0.792   3. 150   4. 0.0000000000936

In problems 5–8 write the number as a decimal.

5. 3.23×10^{-6} 6. 8.5×10^2 7. 7.3765×10^{-3} 8. 2.7945×10^{10}

Decimal Arithmetic

Add and **subtract** decimals the same way you add and subtract whole numbers, except you have to align the decimal points. It's easiest to arrange the numbers vertically to accomplish this. For example, to add 76.23 and 926.5, first attach a zero to the hundredths place of 926.5, so both numbers have the same number of digits to the right of the decimal. Then arrange them vertically with the decimal point aligned:

$$
\begin{array}{r}
76.23 \\
+926.50 \\
\hline
1002.73
\end{array}
$$

Or, subtract 53.79 from 192.4 as follows:

$$
\begin{array}{r}
192.40 \\
-53.79 \\
\hline
138.61
\end{array}
$$

In the following exercises, the problems are arranged horizontally to save space. You can either arrange them vertically with decimal points aligned, or you can align the decimal points "in your mind" and do the adding or subtracting horizontally.

To **multiply** decimals, multiply as though the numbers were whole numbers, and place the decimal point as many places in from the right as the total of the two numbers being multiplied. (The numbers being multiplied are called **factors**.) For example, in 5.1×1.2, first multiply 51 and 12, to get 612. Since each factor has one digit to the right of the decimal, place the decimal point in 612 two places in from the right, getting 6.12.

To **divide** decimals, multiply both dividend and divisor by a power of 10 that will make both whole numbers. For example, in $9.45 \div 2.1$ $(2.1\sqrt{9.45})$, multiply both by 100 (move each decimal point two places to the right). In other words, change the problem to $945 \div 210$ $(210\sqrt{945})$. When you do this long division, you get 4.5, which is also the answer to the original problem.

- To divide decimals, move the decimal point enough places so that both divisor and dividend are whole numbers.

Decimal Arithmetic Practice

Add, subtract, multiply, or divide as indicated.

1. $7.1 + 3.25$	2. $12.478 - 9.53$	3. $112.43 + 39.1$
4. $\$66.10 - \$13.47$	5. $125.52 + 0.97$	6. $80.03 - 42.95$
7. $\$20.00 - \$8.46$	8. $19.00 - 5.7$	9. 3.4×3
10. $\$12.60 \div 3$	11. 2.5×3.2	12. $5.2 \div 0.2$
13. 12×1.25	14. $0.63 \div 21$	15. 7.5×3
16. $20 \div 0.5$	17. $0.15 \times \$30$	18. $2.04 \div 0.04$
19. 1.9×0.2	20. $1.8 \div 0.09$	

Rounding to a Place Value

The idea of rounding a number to a place value is best illustrated by examples. Take the number 4736.

1. Round 4736 to the nearest thousand. You have to determine if 4736 is closest to 1000 or 2000 or 3000 or 4000, etc. You can quickly narrow the search from 4000 or 5000 because 4736 is between these two. Since it is closer to 5000, **4736 rounded to the nearest thousand is 5000**.

2. Round 4736 to the nearest hundred. You can quickly narrow the search from 4700 and 4800 because 4736 is between these two. Since it is closer to 4700, **4736 rounded to the nearest hundred is 4700**.

3. Round 4736 to the nearest ten. You can quickly narrow the search from 4730 to 4740 because 4736 is between these two. Since it is closer to 4740, **4736 rounded to the nearest ten is 4740**.

The idea is similar when rounding a decimal number. Take the number 0.2463, for example.

1. Round 0.2463 to the nearest thousandth. The thousandths place is the third place to the right of the decimal. In this case the digit *6* is in the thousandths place. You can quickly narrow the search from 0.2560 to 0.2470 because 0.2463 is between these two. Since it is closer to 0.2460, **0.2463 rounded to the nearest thousandth is 0.2460 (=0.246)**.
2. Round 0.2463 to the nearest hundredth. The hundredths place is the second place to the right of the decimal. In this case the digit *4* is in the hundredths place. You can quickly narrow the search from 0.2400 to 0.2500 because 0.2463 is between these two. Since it is closer to 0.2500, **0.2463 rounded to the nearest hundredth is 0.2500 (=0.25)**.
3. Round 0.2643 to the nearest tenth. The tenths place is the first place to the right of the decimal. In this case the digit *2* is in the tenths place. You can quickly narrow the search from 0.2000 to 0.3000 because 0.2643 is between these two. Since it is closer to 0.3000, **0.2643 rounded to the nearest tenth is 0.3000 (=0.3)**.

You may be asked to round a decimal number to the nearest unit. Suppose you have to round 0.2643 to the nearest unit. The units place is the first place to the left of the decimal. In this case the digit *0* is in the units place. Therefore, 0.2643 rounds to either 0 or 1. Since it is closer to 0, **0.2643 rounded to the nearest unit is 0**.

Round 38.09 to the nearest unit. The digit *8* is in the units place. You can quickly narrow the search from 38 to 39. Since it is closer to 38, **38.09 rounded to the nearest unit is 38**.

Rule for Rounding to a Place Value

The rule for rounding was shown in the preceding examples. Call the digit in the place value you are rounding to, the *rounding digit*. Look at the digit just to the right of the rounding digit. If this digit is less than 5, leave the rounding digit as is and change the remaining digits to the right to 0. If this digit is 5 or more, increase the rounding digit by 1 and change the remaining digits to the right to 0.

Some problems just ask you to round numbers. For other problems, rounding is only part of the problem. Rounded numbers are used in short-cut calculations to answer questions. These shortcuts are illustrated in the following examples.

Example E. Which of the following is the best estimate of 297.4×10.2?

    a. 6000   **b.** 3000   **c.** 1000   **d.** 30

Round 297.4 to the nearest hundred—300. Round 10.2 to the nearest ten—10. Multiply 300 by 10 to get 3000 (B).

Example F.   Which of these is the best estimate of 5910.8 ÷ 6?

    a. 10   **b.** 100   **c.** 1000   **d.** 10,000

Round 5910.8 to 6000. 6000 ÷ 6 = 1000. The correct answer is C.

Example G.   One month a contractor earns $563, $612, $890, and $392 on four jobs. About how much did the contractor earn on these four jobs?

    a. $2500   **b.** $2400   **c.** $2300   **d.** $2200

Round the numbers to the nearest hundred because the answers are written to that place value. The rounded earnings are $600, $600, $900, and $400. Since all of these are hundreds, just add 6, 6, 9, and 4 mentally to get 25. The correct answer is $2500 (A).

Example H.   Clair rounded the number 8835 to the nearest hundred. Steve rounded this number to the nearest thousand. What was the difference between the two rounded numbers?

    a. 35   **b.** 100   **c.** 150   **d.** 200

To the nearest hundred, 8835 rounds to 8800. To the nearest thousand, 8835 rounds to 9000. The difference between 9000 and 8800 is 200 (D).

Example I.   A wedding ceremony cost $4985. There were 98 guests at the wedding. What was the cost per guest?

    a. $10   **b.** $50   **c.** $100   **d.** $150

Round $4985 to $5000. Round 98 guests to 100 guests. Divide $5000 by 100 to get $50 per guest (B).

Rounding Practice

Round each number to the place value indicated.

1. 58.4 to the nearest unit

2. 0.568 to the nearest hundredth

3. 2354 to the nearest ten

4. 345 to the nearest hundred

5. 0.7205 to the nearest thousandth

6. 0.1643 to the nearest tenth

7. 12.58 to the nearest ten

8. 0.111 to the nearest tenth

9. 1765 to the nearest thousand

10. 17.855 to the nearest hundredth

LESSON 2
FRACTIONS

What Are Fractions?

A fraction is a way of showing **part of a whole**. For example, some say that the weather in New England is cold 5 months out of 12. A fraction can also mean **division**. For example, a party host might divide 5 pizzas equally among 12 people. Each person would get $\frac{5}{12}$ (a little less than half) of a pizza. (It's always better to write a fraction such as five-twelfths as $\frac{5}{12}$ instead of 5/12.)

There are two kinds of fractions. *Proper* fractions have a smaller numerator (top number) than denominator (bottom number). For example, $\frac{5}{12}$ is a proper fraction. Let's just call these "fractions." Fractions that show part of a whole are always proper fractions.

In an *improper* fraction, the numerator is bigger. For example, $\frac{5}{2}$ is an example of an improper fraction. Improper fractions never show part of a whole since a part can never be bigger than the whole. Instead, you can think of an improper fraction as a division problem or a ratio. You can think of the improper fraction $\frac{5}{2}$ as 5 pizzas divided between 2 people ($2\frac{1}{2}$ pizzas each!), or as earning \$5 for every \$2 you spend (ratio).

TABE Level A expects you to be able to interpret fractions as in the examples just given. It also expects you to reduce fractions and to add, subtract, multiply, and divide fractions, mixed numbers, and improper fractions. Explanations of these procedures will be easier if we first look at the connection between improper fractions, whole numbers, and mixed numbers.

Improper Fractions, Whole Numbers, and Mixed Numbers

Whole numbers are really improper fractions in disguise. For example, the whole number 10 and the improper fraction $\frac{10}{1}$ are the same amounts.

- To change a whole number to an improper fraction, just put the whole number in the numerator and 1 in the denominator.

When you put a whole number and a fraction together you get a **mixed number,** such as $5\frac{1}{2}$. Suppose you have a $5\frac{1}{2}$-year-old child. Since 5 years is 10 half-years, this child has lived for 11 half-years, or $\frac{11}{2}$ years.

Changing mixed numbers to improper fractions is best illustrated by examples. Three such examples are shown next:

Example A. Change $6\frac{5}{8}$ to an improper fraction: $6\frac{5}{8} = \frac{8 \times 6 + 5}{8} = \frac{53}{8}$.

Example B. Change $2\frac{3}{5}$ to an improper fraction: $2\frac{3}{5} = \frac{5 \times 2 + 3}{5} = \frac{13}{5}$.

Example C. Change $9\frac{2}{7}$ to an improper fraction: $9\frac{2}{7} = \frac{7 \times 9 + 2}{7} = \frac{65}{7}$.

Changing improper fractions to mixed numbers is the reverse process. Again, examples are the best way to show how to do this.

Example D. Change $\frac{15}{8}$ to a mixed number.
Divide 8 into 15 and get 1, with a remainder of 7: $\frac{15}{8} = 1\frac{7}{8}$.

Example E. Change $\frac{5}{2}$ to a mixed number.
Divide 2 into 5 and get 2, with a remainder of 1: $\frac{5}{2} = 2\frac{1}{2}$.

Example F. Change $\frac{73}{8}$ to a mixed number.
Divide 8 into 73 and get 9, with a remainder of 1: $\frac{73}{8} = 9\frac{1}{8}$.

Practice Changing Between Improper Fractions, Whole Numbers, and Mixed Numbers

Change each improper fraction to a mixed number or whole number.

1. $\frac{4}{3}$ 2. $\frac{7}{4}$ 3. $\frac{6}{5}$ 4. $\frac{8}{3}$ 5. $\frac{9}{3}$ 6. $\frac{5}{1}$

7. $\frac{12}{7}$ 8. $\frac{4}{2}$ 9. $\frac{15}{8}$ 10. $\frac{13}{10}$ 11. $\frac{11}{4}$ 12. $\frac{12}{3}$

Change each mixed number to an improper fraction.

13. $1\frac{2}{3}$ 14. $2\frac{1}{2}$ 15. $4\frac{2}{5}$ 16. $1\frac{11}{12}$ 17. $3\frac{1}{3}$ 18. $6\frac{1}{8}$

19. $8\frac{3}{8}$ 20. $5\frac{7}{9}$ 21. $9\frac{3}{5}$ 22. $8\frac{7}{10}$ 23. $3\frac{5}{9}$ 24. $7\frac{1}{4}$

Reducing Fractions

A fraction can be reduced if the same number divides evenly into both the numerator and the denominator. In the fraction $\frac{9}{12}$, divide both 9 and 12 by 3 to get $\frac{3}{4}$. This is an example of reducing a fraction, and the two fractions are called *equivalent*. Both are equal to the decimal 0.75. If a basketball player makes 3 free throws out of 4 attempts, you would expect that player to make 9 out of 12 attempts. Both describe a "75% free-throw shooter."

- Equivalent fractions have the same value; they just use different numbers.

If you look at the fraction $\frac{12}{30}$, you could divide both 12 and 30 by 2 and reduce it to $\frac{6}{15}$. But then you could divide both 6 and 15 by 3 and reduce again to $\frac{2}{5}$. Only 1 divides evenly into 2 and 5, so this can't be reduced further: $\frac{12}{30}$ has been reduced to lowest terms—namely, $\frac{2}{5}$. This could have been accomplished in one step instead of two by dividing both 12 and 30 by 6, instead of dividing by 2 and then by 3. In general, you can reduce a fraction to lowest terms in one step if you use the largest divisor of both numerator and denominator.

Not all fractions can be reduced. If 1 is the largest number that divides evenly into both its numerator and denominator, a fraction is already in lowest terms. For example, the fraction $\frac{4}{7}$ can't be reduced.

You can reduce improper fractions to lowest terms the same way. Just find the largest number that divides evenly into both numerator and denominator, or divide both by smaller numbers until you can divide numerator and denominator only by 1.

Example G. Reduce $\frac{20}{8}$.

Divide both 20 and 8 by 4: $\frac{20}{8} = \frac{5}{2}$.

If the denominator is 1 after you reduce an improper fraction to lowest terms, it means the denominator divided evenly into the numerator in the first place, and the result is a whole number.

Example H. Reduce $\frac{18}{3}$.

Divide both 18 and 3 by 3: $\frac{18}{3} = \frac{6}{1} = 6$.

Practice Reducing Fractions

Reduce each to lowest terms.

1. $\dfrac{2}{6}$ 2. $\dfrac{5}{10}$ 3. $\dfrac{3}{12}$ 4. $\dfrac{2}{20}$ 5. $\dfrac{10}{15}$ 6. $\dfrac{18}{24}$

7. $\dfrac{15}{10}$ 8. $\dfrac{8}{12}$ 9. $\dfrac{12}{4}$ 10. $\dfrac{6}{16}$ 11. $\dfrac{9}{6}$ 12. $\dfrac{12}{20}$

Multiplying Fractions

Multiplying fractions is easier than adding, subtracting, or dividing them. To multiply two fractions, just multiply the numerators and multiply the denominators. It doesn't matter whether the fractions are proper or improper.

Example I.   Multiply $\dfrac{2}{3} \times \dfrac{4}{7}$: $\dfrac{2}{3} \times \dfrac{4}{7} = \dfrac{2 \times 4}{3 \times 7} = \dfrac{8}{21}$.

Since a whole number can be thought of as a fraction with 1 as the denominator, multiplying a whole number times a fraction is just like multiplying two fractions.

Example J.   Multiply $\dfrac{5}{8}$ by 3: $\dfrac{5}{8} \times 3 = \dfrac{5}{8} \times \dfrac{3}{1} = \dfrac{5 \times 3}{8 \times 1} = \dfrac{15}{8} = 1\dfrac{7}{8}$.

To multiply a fraction by a mixed number, just change the mixed number to an improper fraction and multiply.

Example K.   Multiply $\dfrac{2}{3} \times 1\dfrac{2}{5}$.

Change the mixed number $1\dfrac{1}{5}$ to $1\dfrac{2}{5}$. Then multiply to get $\dfrac{2}{3} \times \dfrac{7}{5} = \dfrac{14}{15}$.

Sometimes when you multiply fractions, the answer is a fraction that can be reduced. For example, if you multiply $\dfrac{2}{3}$ by $\dfrac{3}{10}$, you get $\dfrac{6}{30}$, which can be reduced to $\dfrac{1}{5}$ by dividing both numerator and denominator by 6. It's easier to do the dividing before multiplying. In this example, the numerators are 2 and 3, while the denominators are 3 and 10. You can divide out *either numerator* with *either denominator,* then multiply what's left, like this:

$$\dfrac{{}^{1}2}{{}_{1}3} \times \dfrac{3^{1}}{{}_{5}10} = \dfrac{1 \times 1}{1 \times 5} = \dfrac{1}{5}$$

Practice Multiplying Fractions

Multiply and reduce to lowest terms. Write improper fraction answers as mixed numbers.

1. $\dfrac{2}{5} \times \dfrac{3}{7}$ 2. $\dfrac{3}{8} \times \dfrac{1}{4}$ 3. $\dfrac{2}{7} \times \dfrac{21}{4}$ 4. $\dfrac{1}{3} \times \dfrac{6}{7}$

5. $5 \times \dfrac{3}{4}$ 6. $\dfrac{5}{8} \times 2\dfrac{1}{3}$ 7. $\dfrac{12}{5} \times \dfrac{1}{2}$ 8. $4 \times \dfrac{17}{12}$

9. $3 \times 2\dfrac{1}{5}$ 10. $1\dfrac{3}{4} \times 2\dfrac{1}{2}$ 11. $5\dfrac{2}{3} \times \dfrac{6}{17}$ 12. $\dfrac{7}{11} \times \dfrac{11}{7}$

Dividing Fractions

Once you have mastered multiplying fractions, dividing fractions is easy. First you need to review some division vocabulary. When you divide 24 by 6, 24 is the **dividend** and 6 is the **divisor**. The answer, 4, is called the **quotient**. Remember that 6 is equivalent to the improper fraction $\dfrac{6}{1}$. If you switch the numerator and denominator, you get $\dfrac{1}{6}$. Now multiply 24 by $\dfrac{1}{6}$. Just as before, the quotient is 4. The fraction $\dfrac{1}{6}$ is called the **reciprocal** of 6 (or $\dfrac{6}{1}$). These steps are summarized next:

$$24 \div 6 = 24 \times \frac{1}{6} = \frac{\cancel{24}^{4}}{1} \times \frac{1}{\cancel{6}_{1}} = \frac{4}{1} = 4$$

- To divide, multiply by the reciprocal.

Example L.   Find the quotient in $\dfrac{1}{4} \div \dfrac{2}{3}$.

The dividend is $\dfrac{1}{4}$, and the divisor is $\dfrac{2}{3}$. Multiply $\dfrac{1}{4}$ by $\dfrac{3}{2}$. The answer is $\dfrac{3}{8}$:

$$\frac{1}{4} \div \frac{2}{3} = \frac{1}{4} \times \frac{3}{2} = \frac{3}{8}$$

If either the dividend or the divisor is a whole number or mixed number, first change them to improper fractions.

Example M.   Find the quotient $2\dfrac{1}{3} \div 7$.

Change the mixed number to an improper fraction: $2\dfrac{1}{3} = \dfrac{7}{3}$. Write 7 as $\dfrac{7}{1}$. Divide $\dfrac{7}{3}$ by $\dfrac{7}{1}$. Multiply $\dfrac{7}{3}$ by $\dfrac{1}{7}$. Divide out the 7s. Answer is $\dfrac{1}{3}$.

$$2\frac{1}{3} \div 7 = \frac{7}{3} \div 7 = \frac{7}{3} \div \frac{7}{1} = \frac{\cancel{7}^{1}}{3} \times \frac{1}{\cancel{7}_{1}} = \frac{1}{3}$$

Practice Dividing Fractions

Divide and reduce to lowest terms. Write improper fraction answers as mixed numbers.

1. $\dfrac{2}{5} \div \dfrac{1}{3}$ 2. $\dfrac{5}{8} \div \dfrac{2}{5}$ 3. $\dfrac{12}{7} \div \dfrac{1}{2}$ 4. $\dfrac{4}{7} \div 2$

5. $5 \div \dfrac{5}{9}$ 6. $1\dfrac{1}{2} \div \dfrac{3}{4}$ 7. $12 \div \dfrac{2}{3}$ 8. $2\dfrac{1}{5} \div 1\dfrac{2}{3}$

9. $6 \div 1\dfrac{1}{2}$ 10. $1 \div 3$ 11. $1 \div \dfrac{1}{3}$ 12. $\dfrac{1}{3} \div \dfrac{2}{3}$

Adding and Subtracting Fractions

Unlike multiplying (and dividing) fractions, adding and subtracting them is somewhat more difficult. This is because fractions must have the same denominators in order to add and subtract them. If the fractions in an addition or subtraction problem have the same denominators, then it's very easy. To get the numerator of the answer, add or subtract the numerators of the two fractions. The denominator of the answer is the same as the common denominator of the two fractions. For example:

$$\frac{5}{8} + \frac{7}{8} = \frac{5 + 7}{8} = \frac{12}{8}$$

In this case, the answer can be reduced and, since it's an improper fraction, it can be changed to a mixed number:

$$\frac{^{3}\cancel{12}}{\cancel{8}_{2}} = \frac{3}{2} = 1\frac{1}{2}$$

If the two fractions that are being added or subtracted have different denominators, you need to change them to equivalent fractions that have the same denominator. This is the reverse of the procedure for reducing fractions. Suppose, for example, that you want to add $\dfrac{3}{4}$ to $\dfrac{1}{5}$. Look for the smallest number that both denominators divide evenly into—in this case 20. This is called the **least common denominator**. Four goes into 20 five times, so multiply the 3 by 5 to get $\dfrac{3 \times 5}{4 \times 5} = \dfrac{15}{20}$. Five goes into 20 four times, so multiply the 1 by 4 to get $\dfrac{1 \times 4}{5 \times 4} = \dfrac{4}{20}$. Then add 15 and 4 to get $\dfrac{19}{20}$. To summarize:

$$\frac{3}{4} + \frac{1}{5} = \frac{3 \times 5}{4 \times 5} + \frac{1 \times 4}{5 \times 4} = \frac{15}{20} + \frac{4}{20} = \frac{19}{20}$$

- Before adding or subtracting fractions, be sure you have a common denominator.

The procedure is the same if either of the numbers being added or subtracted is a whole number or a mixed number. Just change to improper fractions and proceed in the same fashion. If the answer can be reduced, you should do that. If the answer is an improper fraction, you can change it to a mixed number or whole number. Here are three more examples to illustrate these points.

Example N.   Add $\frac{2}{3} + \frac{5}{6}$.

Since the two denominators 3 and 6 both divide evenly into 6, the least common denominator is 6. Multiply both numerator and denominator of $\frac{2}{3}$ by 2 to get $\frac{4}{6}$. Add $\frac{4}{6}$ to $\frac{5}{6}$ to get $\frac{9}{6}$. Reduce $\frac{9}{6}$ to $\frac{3}{2}$. Change $\frac{3}{2}$ to the mixed number $1\frac{1}{2}$.

$$\frac{2}{3} + \frac{5}{6} = \frac{2 \times 2}{3 \times 2} + \frac{5}{6} = \frac{4}{6} + \frac{5}{6} = \frac{9}{6} = \frac{3}{2} = 1\frac{1}{2}$$

Example O.   Add $2\frac{2}{3} + 3\frac{1}{2}$.

Change mixed numbers to improper fractions: $2\frac{2}{3} = \frac{8}{3}$ and $3\frac{1}{2} = \frac{7}{2}$. The least common denominator is 6. Multiply $\frac{8}{3}$ by $\frac{2}{2}$ to get $\frac{16}{6}$ and multiply $\frac{7}{2}$ by $\frac{3}{3}$ to get $\frac{21}{6}$. Add $\frac{16}{6}$ and $\frac{21}{6}$ to get $\frac{37}{6}$. Change $\frac{37}{6}$ to the mixed number $6\frac{1}{6}$.

$$2\frac{2}{3} + 3\frac{1}{2} = \frac{8}{3} + \frac{7}{2} = \frac{8 \times 2}{3 \times 2} + \frac{7 \times 3}{2 \times 3} = \frac{16}{6} + \frac{21}{6} = \frac{37}{6} = 6\frac{1}{6}$$

Example P.   Subtract $1\frac{2}{5}$ from 4.

Since 4 is a whole number, there is an easier way to do this problem. It takes $\frac{3}{5}$ to get $1\frac{2}{5}$ up to 2 and 2 more to get to 4. So the answer is $2\frac{3}{5}$. The methods described in the previous paragraphs give the same answer:

$$4 - 1\frac{2}{5} = \frac{4}{1} - \frac{7}{5} = \frac{4 \times 5}{1 \times 5} - \frac{7}{5} = \frac{20}{5} - \frac{7}{5} = \frac{13}{5} = 2\frac{3}{5}$$

Practice Adding and Subtracting Fractions

Add or subtract as indicated. Reduce all fractions and change all improper fractions to whole numbers or mixed numbers.

1. $\frac{1}{5} + \frac{2}{5}$ 2. $\frac{7}{9} - \frac{4}{9}$ 3. $\frac{1}{2} + \frac{1}{3}$ 4. $\frac{7}{8} - \frac{1}{4}$

5. $\frac{2}{3} + \frac{1}{5}$ 6. $\frac{3}{4} - \frac{3}{10}$ 7. $3 + \frac{7}{5}$ 8. $4\frac{2}{3} - 2\frac{1}{2}$

9. $8\frac{3}{8} + 2\frac{5}{12}$ 10. $2\frac{1}{3} - \frac{3}{5}$ 11. $4\frac{2}{3} + 2\frac{1}{3}$ 12. $1\frac{1}{2} - \frac{3}{5}$

Changing Between Fractions and Decimals

To change a fraction to a decimal, divide the numerator by the denominator. A fraction such as $\frac{5}{8}$ is a number, but it is also a division problem. If you divide 8 into 5 (or equivalently, divide 5 by 8), you get 0.625, a decimal. Therefore, $\frac{5}{8}$ and 0.625 are just different names for the same number. The **fraction form** is $\frac{5}{8}$, and the **decimal form** is 0.625.

Sometimes when you divide, you get a never-ending repeating decimal. For example, $\frac{1}{3} = .333 \ldots$. You can write a repeating decimal by writing the repeating part once and putting a line over it. For example, $\frac{1}{3} = 0.\overline{3}$. Or, you can round off according to the requirements of a problem.

To change a **decimal to a fraction**, move the decimal point to make the decimal a whole number. This whole number is the numerator of the fraction, and the denominator is a 1 followed by the number of places you moved the decimal.

Example Q.   Change 0.4572 to a fraction.

Move the decimal point four places to the right to get 4572. The denominator is 10,000. So the fraction is $\frac{4572}{10,000}$.

Example R.   Change 18.05 to a fraction.

Move the decimal point two places to the right to get 1805. The denominator is 100. So the fraction is $\frac{1805}{100}$.

Practice Changing Between Fractions and Decimals

Change each fraction to a decimal. If necessary, round your answer to the nearest hundredth.

1. $\dfrac{1}{4}$ 2. $\dfrac{2}{3}$ 3. $\dfrac{7}{8}$ 4. $\dfrac{4}{5}$ 5. $\dfrac{9}{12}$ 6. $\dfrac{6}{7}$

Change each decimal to a fraction. Reduce your answer to lowest terms.

7. 0.6   8. 0.28   9. 0.65   10. 0.125   11. 0.92   12. 1.5

What Are Integers?

Whole numbers are 0, 1, 2, 3, . . ., and so on, forever. Their opposites are ⁻1, ⁻2, ⁻3, . . . (negative 1, negative 2, negative 3, and so forth), forever. These positive and negative whole numbers and zero are called **integers**. Most of the numbers you use in day-to-day life are positive. However, negative numbers have an important place in real life as well. When someone owes you money, it is a positive amount. When you owe someone else money, it is a negative amount. When a football team gains yards, it is positive yardage. When the team loses yards, it is negative yardage. There are temperatures above zero and below zero. Land may be above sea level (positive) or below sea level (negative).

It is useful to think of integers as the marks on an outdoor thermometer held sideways. Zero is in the middle. Positive integers go right and negative integers go left.

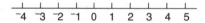

The mathematical name for this figure is the **number line**. The number line is a picture of all numbers, including positive and negative fractions, integers, and other numbers called *irrational numbers*. The only irrational number you need to know about for the TABE A is the number π (pi), covered in Lesson 9.

An integer and its **opposite** are the same distance from zero. They just go in opposite directions. For example, 3 and ⁻3 are both 3 away from 0, but 3 goes to the right while ⁻3 goes to the left.

TABE A follows certain conventions for writing positive and negative numbers:

1. If a number is positive, it doesn't have a + sign in front of it. Whenever you see a +, it means "plus" or "add."
2. If a number is negative, it has a raised minus sign (⁻) in front of it, as in ⁻5.

Let's see how to read some examples.

Example A. ⁻1 + 5: negative one plus five

Example B. ⁻7 + ⁻6: negative seven plus negative six

Example C. 4 + ⁻3: four plus negative three

Example D. 5 − 8: five minus eight

Example E. ⁻3 − 9: negative three minus nine

Example F. 2 − ⁻6: two minus negative six

Example G. ⁻3 − ⁻7: negative three minus negative seven

This is part of the language of math. You need to make sure you know how to read math correctly.

You need to be able to add, subtract, multiply, and divide integers on the TABE A.

Adding Integers

If two integers are both positive, just add them like whole numbers. If they are both negative, ignore the sign, add them, and put a negative sign in front of the answer. For example, 6 + 2 = 8 and ⁻6 = ⁻2 = ⁻8. If two integers have *different* signs, follow these steps:

1. Ignore the signs. In other words, look at the **absolute values** of the two numbers.
2. Subtract the smaller absolute value from the larger one.
3. Attach the negative sign to the answer if the larger absolute value was originally negative. Otherwise, the answer is positive.

Example H. 8 + ⁻3

1. Ignore the signs (absolute values): 8, 3.
2. Subtract the smaller absolute value (3) from the larger one (8): 8 − 3 = 5.
3. Since the larger absolute value is 8, the answer is positive 5, or just 5.

Example I. ⁻12 + 3

1. Ignore the signs: 12, 3.
2. Subtract the smaller absolute value (3) from the larger one (12): 12 − 3 = 9.
3. Attach the negative sign, because the larger absolute value (12) is negative. The answer is ⁻9.

Practice Adding Integers

Add as indicated.

1. $^-4 + 8$ 2. $5 + {}^-8$ 3. $^-6 + {}^-14$ 4. $7 + {}^-5$

5. $^-3 + 1$ 6. $^-7 + {}^-4$ 7. $1 + {}^-1$ 8. $^-3 + 6$

Subtracting Integers

The word "subtract" (or "minus") means "add the opposite." For example, $5 - 7$ (5 **minus** 7) means $5 + {}^-7$, add 5 and negative 7.

- Change a subtraction problem to an addition problem by adding the opposite.

Examples J. $^-6 - 2$ means $^-6 + {}^-2$ because $^-2$ is the opposite of 2.

Example K. $4 - {}^-10$ means $4 + 10$ because 10 is the opposite of $^-10$.

Example L. $9 - 12$ means $9 + {}^-12$ because $^-12$ is the opposite of 12.

Example M. $15 - {}^-8$ means $15 + 8$ because 8 is the opposite of $^-8$.

Practice Subtracting Integers

Subtract as indicated.

1. $8 - {}^-3$ 2. $^-4 - 13$ 3. $^-1 - {}^-8$ 4. $12 - {}^-1$

5. $3 - 15$ 6. $^-7 - {}^-2$ 7. $12 - 4$ 8. $6 - {}^-6$

Multiplying and Dividing Integers

Multiplying and dividing integers is easy. Just multiply or divide as you would with whole numbers. If the numbers have the *same* sign (both positive or both negative), the answer is positive. If the numbers have *different signs,* the answer is negative.

Example N. $^-6 \times 4 = {}^-24$

Example O. $3 \times {}^-15 = {}^-45$

Example P. $^-2 \times {}^-4 = 8$

Example Q. $18 \div {}^-3 = {}^-6$

Example R. $25 \div {}^-5 = {}^-5$

Example S. $^-12 \div {}^-2 = 6$

- Make sure you know whether you are multiplying or adding before using the same sign/opposite sign rule.

Practice Multiplying and Dividing Integers

Multiply as indicated.

1. $^-7 \times 4$

2. $15 \div ^-3$

3. $9 \times ^-22$

4. $^-63 \div 7$

5. $^-13 \times ^-4$

6. $^-66 \div 11$

7. $3 \times ^-9$

8. $^-54 \div ^-6$

9. $72 \div ^-12$

Mixed Practice on Integers

Perform the indicated operation.

1. $21 - ^-8$

2. $^-35 \div 7$

3. $^-19 + ^-6$

4. $^-20 \div ^-5$

5. $^-32 - ^-8$

6. $^-3 \times ^-7$

7. $^-9 + ^-13$

8. $42 \times ^-1$

9. $^-7 + 12$

LESSON 4 | PERCENT

What Are Percents?

Percents are all around us. A department store has a 15% off sale. You can finance a car at 5% interest. A basketball player has a 46% shooting average. You score 80% on your test. You leave a 15% or 20% tip after eating a meal in a restaurant. In all these examples, percent is a way of measuring **part of a whole**.

The department store sale saves you *part of the whole* cost of what you buy. The interest is the *part of the total* amount of money you borrow that you have to pay back (in addition to repaying the borrowed money). The free throw average is the *part of all* the free throws the player takes. The test score is *part of all* the questions that you got right. Percents give you an idea of how much of the whole the part is, regardless of how many things there are or what they are. A score of 80% on a test could be 8 correct answers out of 10 questions or 20 correct out of 25 questions. A 46% shooting average could be 46 shots made out of 100 taken, or 23 made out of 50 taken. The 15% off sale could mean that you save $4.50 on a $30 jacket or $75 on a $500 TV set. This is because the part is **standardized** to a whole of 100.

Common percents are 50%, 25%, and 10%. Fifty percent of a number is just half of that number, while 25% is a quarter of the number (half of a half). To find 10% of a number, just move the decimal point one place to the left.

You also occasionally hear of percents bigger than 100%. In this case the "part" is actually larger than the whole. It is not unusual for a coach to say that one of his players gave 110% in a game, implying that the player really hustled. Percents over 100% are also occasionally used to dramatize a change. For example, you might hear that gasoline prices are 300% of what they were 10 years ago, or that they are 200% greater than they were (both mean the same thing).

Solving Basic Percent Problems

Percent problems ask you to find one of three numbers.

1. The problem tells you the whole and the part, and you have to find the %.
2. The problem tells you the whole and the %, and you have to find the part.
3. The problem tells you the part and the %, and you have to find the whole.

Whether the "part" is smaller or larger than the whole, there is a formula for each type of problem:

1. $\% = Part \div Whole \times 100$

   - To get the %, divide the part by the whole, and then multiply by 100 (move the decimal point two places to the right).

2. $Part = \% \times Whole \div 100$

   - To get the part, multiply the % by the whole, and then divide by 100 (move the decimal point two places to the left).

3. $Whole = Part \div \% \times 100$

   - To get the whole, divide the part by the %, and then multiply by 100 (move the decimal point two places to the right).

Once you've memorized these formulas, you need to be able to determine which two numbers a problem tells you. This isn't too hard. The number that is in front of the % sign is the %. The number that comes after the word "of" is the whole. The number that comes after the word "is" or "=" is the part. Let's look at an example of each of these.

Example A. What is 20% of 50?

The problem tells you the % and the whole, so use the formula for the part:

$Part = 20 \times 50 \div 100 = 1000 \div 100 = 10$. 20% of 50 is *10*.

Example B. What percent of 30 is 12?

The problem tells you the whole and the part, so use the formula for the %:

$\% = Part \div Whole \times 100 = 12 \div 30 \times 100 = 40$. 12 is *40%* of 30.

Example C. Three is 30% of what number?

The problem tells you the part and the %, so use the formula for the whole:

$Whole = Part \div \% \times 100 = 3 \div 30 \times 100 = 10$. 3 is 30% of *10*.

- The word **of** means **times**.
- The word **is** means **equals**.

Practice Solving Basic Percent Problems

1. Find 12% of 50.

2. What percent of 20 is 9?

3. 10 is 25% of what number?

4. What percent of 10 is 7?

5. 15% of what number is 9?

6. 8% of 300 is_____.

7. What percent of 18 is 9?   8. 12 is 20% of what number?

9. 7 is 25% of what number?   10. Find 90% of 150.

"Decimals," "fractions," and "percents" are just different names for the same group of numbers. If you are told one name of a number, you should be able to determine the other two.

Changing Between Percents and Decimals or Fractions

To change a **decimal to a percent**, just move the decimal point two places to the right (multiply by 100).

Example D.   Change 0.537 to a percent.

Moving the decimal point two places to the right produces the number 53.7, so the answer is 53.7%.

To **change a percent to a decimal**, move the decimal point two places to the left (divide by 100).

Example E.   Change 4.5% to a decimal.

Moving the decimal point two places to the left produces the number 0.045.

Changing a **fraction to a percent** takes two steps. First change the fraction to a decimal by dividing the numerator by the denominator. Then move the decimal point two places to the right as described earlier.

Example F.   Change $\frac{3}{5}$ to a percent.

First divide 5 into 3 to get 0.6. Then move the decimal two places to the right to get 60. The answer is 60%.

To change a **percent to a fraction** also takes two steps. First, change the percent to a decimal by moving the decimal points two places to the left. Then write the decimal as a fraction.

Example G.   Change 35.6% to a fraction.

As a decimal, 35.6% is 0.356. As a fraction, 0.356 is $\frac{356}{1000}$.

Practice Changing Between Percents
and Decimals and Fractions

Change each to a percent. If necessary, round your answer to the nearest hundredth of a percent.

1. 0.52   2. $\frac{1}{8}$ 3. 0.007

4. $\frac{1}{6}$ 5. 1.25   6. $\frac{13}{25}$

7. 0.035   8. $\dfrac{2}{9}$ 9. 0.084

10. $\dfrac{3}{2}$ 11. 0.0095   12. $\dfrac{4}{10}$

Change each percent to a decimal.

13. 26%   14. 8%   15. 79.2%

16. 2.5%   17. 130%   18. 0.04%

Change each percent to a fraction.

19. 12%   20. 9%   21. 125%

22. 6.5%   23. 0.1%   24. 85.5%

OPERATIONS

What Are Operations?

In math, you can add, subtract, multiply, or divide. These are called **operations**. Each of these involves "operating" on two numbers together to get a single number result. These operations are illustrated in the following examples:

- *Addition:* Add 3 and 6 (3 + 6) with the result 9. The result of adding is called a **sum**.
- *Subtraction:* Subtract 12 from 15 (15 − 12) with the result 3. The result of subtracting is called a **difference**.
- *Multiplication:* Multiply 4 by 8 (8 × 4) with the result 32. The result of multiplying is called a **product**. The numbers that are multiplied are called **factors**.
- *Division:* Divide 20 by 4 (20 ÷ 4) with the result 5. The result of dividing is called a **quotient**. In this example, 4 is the **divisor** and 20 is the **dividend**.

Raising a number to a power is another type of operation. You learned about exponents in Lesson 1 on decimals. An exponent tells you how many times the base is a factor.

For example, 2^3 means the base 2 is a factor 3 times. This results in the number 8 because $2 \times 2 \times 2 = 8$. You read 2^3 as "2 to the 3rd power."

When you raise numbers to the power 2, you **square** the numbers. For example, when you write 4^2, you can read it as "four to the second power," "the square of 4," or "four squared." Squaring a number is special type of raising a number to a power and as such is also an operation.

When you raise a number to the power 1, you don't do anything to it. In other words, $x^1 = x$. As you will see in the next lesson, it's sometimes convenient to think of x as x^1.

Each of the examples, $3 + 6$, $15 - 12$, 8×4, $20 \div 4$, 2^3, and 4^2, is an **expression**. You **evaluate the expression** when you perform the operation indicated to get a single number.

Inverse Operations

Adding and subtracting are actually **inverse** operations. Start, for example, with the number 5. Add 3, and you get 8. Then subtract 3 from 8. You are back to 5. Adding and subtracting are inverse operations because they take you back to where you started.

Multiplication and division are also inverse operations. Start with the number 3. Multiply by 6 and you get 18. Then divide 18 by 6. You are back to 3. Multiplication and division are inverse operations because they take you back to where you started.

Squaring a number also has an inverse operation, called taking the **square root**. Start with the number 7. Square 7 to get 49 ($7^2 = 49$). When you take the square root of 49, you get back to 7. The square root of 49 is 7. The math symbol for "the square root of" is $\sqrt{\ }$, so $\sqrt{49} = 7$. The squares and square roots of the first 12 whole numbers are listed next:

$1^2 = 1$ so $\sqrt{1} = 1$ $\qquad\qquad$ $7^2 = 49$ so $\sqrt{49} = 7$

$2^2 = 4$ so $\sqrt{4} = 2$ $\qquad\qquad$ $8^2 = 64$ so $\sqrt{64} = 8$

$3^2 = 9$ so $\sqrt{9} = 3$ $\qquad\qquad$ $9^2 = 81$ so $\sqrt{81} = 9$

$4^2 = 16$ so $\sqrt{16} = 4$ $\qquad\qquad$ $10^2 = 100$ so $\sqrt{100} = 10$

$5^2 = 25$ so $\sqrt{25} = 5$ $\qquad\qquad$ $11^2 = 121$ so $\sqrt{121} = 11$

$6^2 = 36$ so $\sqrt{36} = 6$ $\qquad\qquad$ $12^2 = 144$ so $\sqrt{144} = 12$

Order of Operations

Addition, subtraction, multiplication, and division are examples of **binary operations** because they operate on two numbers to make one number. What do you do when you want to use more than one operation? For example, you may want to add 4 to 3 and multiply the result by 5. The answer would be 35 (5 times 7). Use parentheses to indicate $(3 + 4)$ as the result of adding 4 to 3. To show that you multiply the result by 5, write $5 \times (3 + 4)$ or $(3 + 4) \times 5$.

You would get a different answer for $(5 \times 3) + 4$, even though the numbers and operations are the same. In this case, you multiply 5 by 3 first, getting 15, and then add 4 to get the answer 19. The lesson here is the importance of parentheses as **grouping symbols**. They show how to apply binary operations to pairs of numbers.

If you want to write a long chain of operations on several numbers, using parentheses can become quite cumbersome. Mathematicians have established a convention for the order of doing operations when there are two or more operations. An expression that is evaluated using this order of operations will always have the same result.

1. Do all the operations in parentheses before you combine the result with other operations. Square roots act like parentheses—do whatever is under the square root before taking the square root. Division bars (fraction bars) also act like parentheses—do whatever is in the numerator and denominator before dividing.

2. Do all exponent operations.

3. Do multiplication and division together, left to right. Multiplication and division are done together because they are inverse operations.

4. Do addition and subtraction together, left to right. Addition and subtraction are done together because they are inverse operations.

Following these rules for $5 \times 3 + 4$, you multiply 5 times 3 to get 15, and then add 4, getting 19. If you meant for the answer to be 35, you would have had to use parentheses and write $5 \times (3 + 4)$.

"**P**lease **E**xcuse **M**y **D**ear **A**unt **S**ally" is a mnemonic to help you remember PEMDAS, an acronym for the correct order of operations. **P** stands for **parentheses**; **E** stands for **exponents**; **M** stands for **multiplication**; **D** stands for **division**; **A** stands for **addition**; and **S** stands for **subtraction**.

There is also an important *notational convention* that is observed when writing expressions with more than one operation. When a number is simply written in front of an expression in parentheses, multiplication is implied. For example, $2(6 + 3)$ means $2 \times (6 + 3)$. Following the order of operations, first add 6 and 3 (in parentheses) to get 9 and then multiply this result by 2 to get 18.

Also, you can show multiplication by writing the numbers next to each other in parentheses: $(4)(7)$ means 4×7.

Following the order of operations may seem difficult or confusing at first but with practice becomes very natural. Several examples are provided next.

Example A.   Evaluate $(4 + 3) \times 2$.

The parentheses indicate that 4 and 3 should be added before multiplying by 2. The answer is 14.

Example B.   Evaluate $5 + 3^2$.

The exponent 2 should be applied first. Then add 5 to the result. The answer is 14. Compare this to $(5 + 3)^2$. Here, the 5 and 3 should be added to get 8. Then square 8 to get the answer 64.

Example C.   Evaluate $3 + 2(4 - 1)$.

In this example, subtract 1 from 4 to get 3 (in parentheses). Then multiply 2 times 3 to get 6. Finally, add 3 to get 9. This example can fool many into first adding 2 and 3 to get 5, and then multiplying 5 by 3 $(4 - 1)$ to get 15.

Example D. Evaluate $\sqrt{9 + 16}$.

It is easy to make an error in this example as well. Since $\sqrt{}$ acts like parentheses, you add 9 and 16 before taking the square root, resulting in $\sqrt{25}$, or 5. If you added $\sqrt{9}$ and $\sqrt{16}$, you would get 3 + 4, or 7, which is incorrect.

Example E. Evaluate $7 - 3 + 2$.

Addition and subtraction are done in left-to-right order. Subtract 3 from 7 to get 4, and add 2 to get 6. Compare this to $7 - (3 + 2)$, where 3 and 2 are added first (parentheses) to get 5, and then 5 is subtracted from 7, resulting in 2.

Example F. Evaluate $6(7 - 4)$.

First subtract 4 from 7 to get 3. Then multiply 3 by 6 to get 18.

All of the examples use positive whole numbers in the expressions and evaluate to positive whole numbers. The order of operations and notational convention apply to all types of numbers: fractions, decimals, or negative numbers. In principle, a problem could ask you to simplify expressions such as $-3(4 - {}^-8)$ or $\left(\dfrac{1}{3} + \dfrac{1}{2} \right) \div 2$.

Practice Using Order of Operations

Follow the order of operations to evaluate each expression.

1. $1 + 6 \times 2$
2. $5^2 \times 3 - 1$
3. $12 \div 2 \times 3$
4. $(5 - 2) \times 4$
5. $9 - (2 + 3)$
6. $3(8 + 2^3)$
7. $3 \times 8 + 2^3$
8. $\sqrt{25 - 16}$
9. $\sqrt{25} - \sqrt{16}$
10. $5 + 3(7 + 1)$
11. $1 + 12 - 9 \div 3 \times 4$
12. $3^2 + 7^2$

What Are Expressions?

In algebra, letters such as a, b, x, or y are used to stand for numbers. To show that you are adding two numbers, just write $a + b$ (or any two letters). To show that you're subtracting one number b from another number a, write $a - b$. To show that you're multiplying two numbers x and y, write xy. To show that you're dividing a number p by a number q, write the fraction form $\frac{p}{q}$. To show that you're raising x to the exponent m, write x^m. The square root of a number is written as $\sqrt{x}$.

The symbols in the previous paragraph are also called **expressions**. Expressions that have letters in them are called **algebraic expressions**. This distinguishes them from **numerical expressions**—those that consist only of numbers. The letters in an algebraic expression are called **variables**.

As with the numerical expressions described in the previous lesson, more than one operation may be involved. For example, $a + b - ab$ is an expression involving the three operations $+$, $-$, and $\times$. Remember that a and b stand for numbers. According to the order of operations, you should first multiply a times b. The result is ab. Then you should add b to a and subtract ab.

Evaluating Expressions

When a problem has an expression and tells you what number each variable stands for, you can be asked to **evaluate** the expression. This means you should **substitute** the number for the variable (replace each variable by the number it stands for) and then evaluate the expression following the order of operations as described in Lesson 5 to do the computations.

A letter that appears in a problem more than once always stands for the same number in that problem. Take, for example, $a^2 + ax$. If a stands for the number 6, and x stands for the number 2, $a^2 + ax$ stands for the number $6^2 + 6 \times 2$, which is $36 + 12$, or 48.

Practice Evaluating Expressions

Suppose $u = 5$, $v = {}^-1$, $w = 3$, and $x = 0.4$. Evaluate each.

1. $u + v$ 2. wx 3. w^2 4. xv

5. $\dfrac{u}{x}$ 6. $w - v$ 7. $w^2 + x$ 8. $(uv)w$

9. $\dfrac{u}{v} - w$ 10. $v^2 - x$ 11. $5x + u$ 12. $2u - v$

Recognizing Properties

Algebra gives us a way of stating what we know about numbers. For instance, we know that you can add two numbers in any order and get the same answer—for example, $5 + 6 = 6 + 5$. But this holds true for *any* two numbers. So we can write $a + b = b + a$ for any two numbers a and b. (*a* and *b* can be the same or different numbers.) This is called the **commutative property of addition**. This same property also holds for multiplication: $ab = ba$ for any two numbers a and b. This is called the **commutative property of multiplication**. One way to remember the word "commutative" is when you commute to work, you go one way (*a* to *b*) and return (*b* to *a*). Note that subtraction does not have the commutative property. For example, $10 - 6 = 4$ but $6 - 10 = {}^-4$.

A second property that also holds for addition and multiplication is the **associative property**. An example of this property for addition is $(5 + 2) + 3 = 5 + (2 + 3)$. This property recognizes that you can add only two numbers at a time. So if you want to add three numbers, you can either add the first two, followed by the third, or you can add the second and third numbers, and then add the result to the first. In both cases the result is 10—you get the same result regardless of which two numbers are *associated*.

An example for multiplication is $(2 \times 3) \times 6 = 2 \times (3 \times 6)$. The result is 36 regardless of which two numbers are associated. To not have to use specific numbers, you can write the associative properties of addition and multiplication as $(a + b) + c = a + (b + c)$ and $(ab)c = a(bc)$ for any numbers a, b, and c.

There is one other important property that combines addition and multiplication. If you add the numbers 4 and 5, then multiply the result by 3, you get 27. Now let's write this as a mathematical statement. First add 4 and 5 and then multiply by 3: $3 \times (4 + 5) = 27$. The fact that you are adding 4 plus 5 first dictates the use of parentheses here. (Without parentheses $3 \times 4 + 5 = 17$.) Now multiply 3 times 4 (12) and 3 times 5 (15). Then add 12 and 15; you get 27, the same result.

This is an example of the **distributive property** (of multiplication over addition): $3 \times (4 + 5) = (3 \times 4) + (3 \times 5)$. The number *3* is *distributed* over 4 and 5. The distributive property holds for any three numbers a, b, and c: $a(b + c) = ab + ac$. (Remember, you don't have to write $\times$ to indicate multiplication when you use letters.) The distributive property of multiplication over *subtraction* also holds: $a(b - c) = ab - ac$.

The following chart summarizes these properties:

Name	Property
Commutative Property of Addition	$a + b = b + a$
Commutative Property of Multiplication	$ab = ba$
Associative Property of Addition	$(a + b) + c = a + (b + c)$
Associative Property of Multiplication	$(ab)c = a(bc)$
Distributive Property over Addition	$a(b + c) = ab + ac$
Distributive Property over Subtraction	$a(b - c) = ab - ac$

Practice Recognizing Properties

Which property is illustrated by each mathematical sentence?

1. $x + 5 = 5 + x$
2. $3(y - 4) = 3y - 12$
3. $1 + (2 + 3) = 1 + (3 + 2)$
4. $(x + y) + 1 = x + (y + 1)$
5. $x (x + 6) = x^2 + 6x$
6. $5(8x) = 40x$

Simplifying Expressions

You can add or subtract expressions that consist of products and quotients to form larger expressions. The expression $3x$ consists of the factors 3 and x, and the expression $5x$ consists of the factors 5 and x. For example, $3x$ and $5x$ consist of the products 3 times x and 5 times x. Add these to form the larger expression $3x + 5x$. As parts of the larger expression, $3x$ and $5x$ are called **terms**. The numbers *3* and *5* are called **coefficients**. When terms have the same variable raised to the same power, they are called **like terms**: $3x$ and $5x$ are like terms. So are $9x^2$ and $4x^2$. But $2x$ and y are *not* like terms because the variables are different. Neither are $3x^4$ and $7x^3$ because the exponents are different.

- To be like terms, terms must both be numbers or must have the same variable to the same power.

You can simplify expressions when the terms are like terms. For example, you can simplify $3x + 5x$. According the Distributive Property, $3x + 5x = (3 + 5)x = 8x$. So to simplify a sum or difference of like terms, just add or subtract the coefficients.

When you multiply a number by 1, the result is the same as the number. Therefore $1x$ and x are the same quantity. This means, for example, $4x + x = 4x + 1x$, which simplifies to $5x$.

When you multiply a number by $^-1$, the result is the opposite of the number. Therefore ^-1x and ^-x are the same quantity. This means, for example, $4x - x = 4x + {}^-1x = 3x$.

When two different variables are used in the same problem, you should assume that they stand for different numbers. Thus, it is not possible to simplify an expression such as $3x + 5y$. In an expression such as this, $3x$ and $5y$ are said to be **unlike terms**.

You may also be able to simplify the product of two expressions. For example, to show that you're multiplying $2u$ and $8u$, write $(2u)(8u)$. In this context, the expressions $2u$ and $8u$ are *not* called terms of the larger expression because they are multiplied, not added. If you apply the commutative and associative properties of multiplication several times, you can write this $(2 \times 8)(u \times u)$ instead of $(2u)(8u)$, and this simplifies to $16u^2$.

- The only time you can get a power of a variable is if you multiply the variable by itself.

Let's look at some more examples that simplify products of expressions involving exponents.

Example A.   Simplify x^3x^5.

Since $x^3 = x \times x \times x$ and $x^5 = x \times x \times x \times x \times x$, $x^3x^5 = (x \times x \times x)(x \times x \times x \times x \times x) = x^8$.

- If you're multiplying two expressions with the same base, add the exponents. This rule also works when there is "no exponent." Recall that $x = x^1$, so, for example, $x \times x^3 = x^4$ because $1 + 3 = 4$.

Example B.   Simplify $(y^2)^3$.

The order of operations says that y^2 is a factor 3 times: $(y^2)(y^2)(y^2)$. Example A says add the exponents, but instead of adding $2 + 2 + 2$, just multiply 3×2, so $(y^2)^3 = y^6$.

- If you have a "power to a power," multiply the powers.

Example C.   Fact: $(ab)^3 = a^3b^3$.

According to the order of operations, $(ab)^3$ means $(ab)(ab)(ab)$. Because multiplication can be done in any order, this is equal to $(a \times a \times a)(b \times b \times b) = a^3b^3$.

- The power of a product is the product of the powers.

Practice Simplifying Expressions

Simplify each expression if possible.

1. $7p - 3p$ 2. $(7p)(3p)$ 3. x^2x^5 4. $9x^2 + 3x^2$

5. $8(3x)$ 6. $(y^2)^4$ 7. $u^2 - v^2$ 8. $15x^5 - 11x^5$

9. $(u^2v^3)^4$ 10. $6 - 2x$ 11. $5y^3 - y^3$ 12. $5x^2 + 4x$

Solving Equations

Equations are math sentences. The equation $4 + 3 = 7$ is true, but the equation $5 - 3 = 6$ is false. In algebra, equations have variables in them. For example, to express the idea that 3 times a number is 12, you write $3x = 12$. Whether this equation is true or false depends on what number is substituted for x. If you substitute 4 for x, this equation is true because $3 \times 4 = 12$, and the number 4 is called a **solution** to this equation. You may be asked to **solve equations** on the TABE A. This means to find a number that makes the equation true.

When you solve an equation, you find a *solution* (number that makes the equation true when substituted for the variable). Many one-operation equations can be solved by the "guess and check" method. With this method, you simply guess the solution, substitute it for the variable, and see if the resulting equation is true.

Example D. Solve $x + 4 = 7$.

This problem asks what number plus 4 equals 7. The answer is 3, so $x = 3$.

Example E. Solve $x - 7 = 4$.

This problem asks what number you subtract 7 from to get 4. The answer is $x = 11$.

Example F. Solve $4x = 24$.

This problem asks what number multiplied by 4 makes 24. The answer is $x = 6$.

Example G. Solve $\frac{x}{3} = 5$.

This problem asks what number divided by 3 makes 5. The answer is $x = 15$.

One-operation equations, however, might involve negative numbers, fractions, or decimals.

Example H. Solve $x + 12 = 9$.

If you can add integers in your head, you will see that the correct answer is $x = {}^-3$.

Example I. Solve $14x = 7$.

This problem asks what number times 14 makes 7. The answer is $x = \frac{1}{2}$ or $x = .5$.

Example J. Solve $x - {}^-6 = {}^-4$.

This problem asks what number ${}^-6$ must be subtracted from to make ${}^-4$. This problem is more difficult, but the answer is ${}^-10$ because ${}^-10 - {}^-6 = {}^-10 + 6 = {}^-4$.

There is another method for solving equations, especially when more than one operation is involved. Let's first see how this method applies when there is only one operation. Solve the equation $x + 7 = 12$. You can *isolate* the variable x by subtracting 7 from $x + 7$ because $x + 7 - 7 = x$. But to keep the equation **balanced**, you must subtract 7 from its other side. This is shown in the steps:

$$x + 7 \underline{- 7} = 12 \underline{- 7}$$
$$x = 5$$

Now solve the equation $7x = 42$. Recall that $7x$ means 7 times x. Since division is the inverse of multiplication, divide both sides of the equation by 7:

$$7x = 42$$

$$\frac{7x}{7} = \frac{42}{7}$$

$$x = 6$$

When you divide the left side of the equation by 7, you return to the original quantity x. To balance the equation, you must also divide the other side of the equation by 7, and $\frac{42}{7} = 6$.

Suppose you have an equation that has two operations. For example, solve $3x + 4 = 10$. First, subtract 4 from both sides of the equation to get $3x = 6$. Then divide both sides of the equation by 3 to get $x = 2$.

$$3x + 4 \underline{- 4} = 10 \underline{- 4}$$
$$3x = 6$$
$$\frac{3x}{3} = \frac{6}{3}$$
$$x = 2$$

The two steps have to be done in this order. If you tried to divide by 3 first, you would have had to divide $3x + 4$ by 3, and this would *not* have left you with $x + 4$, so you wouldn't be able to find the value of x by subtraction. Notice that the two steps were subtraction, followed by division— *reversing* the order of operations.

Reversing the order of operations makes sense because you are undoing things that have been "done" to x. In the example just shown, you can think of starting with some unknown number x. When you multiply by 3 and add 4, you get the answer 10. To get back to x, reverse the steps: subtract 4 and divide by 3.

There are *two basic principles* you must follow in order to solve equations: (1) use what you know about inverse operations (addition/subtraction and multiplication/division) to isolate the variable; and (2) keep the equation balanced (do the same thing to both sides).

Now let's look at a few more examples of solving equations.

Example K.   Solve $\frac{x}{3} = 7$.

The equation says x divided by 3 is equal to 7. Since the inverse of division is multiplication, multiply both sides of the equation by 3.

$$\frac{x}{3} = 7$$

$$\underline{3} \times \frac{x}{3} = \underline{3} \times 7$$

$$x = 21$$

Example L.   Solve $6x - 13 = 11$.

Add 13 to both sides of the equation. Then divide both sides of the equation by 6.

$$6x - 13 \underline{+ 13} = 11 \underline{+ 13}$$

$$6x = 24$$

$$\frac{6x}{6} = \frac{24}{6}$$

$$x = 4$$

Example M.   Solve $\frac{x}{2} + 5 = 8$.

Subtract 5 from both sides of the equation. Then multiply both sides of the equation by 2.

$$\frac{x}{2} + 5 \underline{- 5} = 8 \underline{- 5}$$

$$\frac{x}{2} = 3$$

$$\underline{2} \times \frac{x}{2} = \underline{2} \times 3$$

$$x = 6$$

Equations can have solutions that are fractions.

Example N.   Solve $12x - 3 = 4$.

Add 3 to both sides of the equation. Then divide both sides of the equation by 12.

$$12x - 3 = 4$$

$$12x - 3 \underline{+ 3} = 4 \underline{+ 3}$$

$$12x = 7$$

$$\frac{12x}{12} = \frac{7}{12}$$

$$x = \frac{7}{12}$$

The solution is $\frac{7}{12}$. In decimal form this number is .58333 . . ..

Example O. $18 - 5x = 3$.

Add $5x$ to both sides of the equation. Subtract 3 from both sides of the equation. Finally, divide both sides of the equation by 5.

$$18 - 5x = 3$$

$$18 - 5x \underline{+ 5x} = 3 \underline{+ 5x}$$

$$18 = 3 + 5x$$

$$18 \underline{- 3} = 3 + 5x \underline{- 3}$$

$$15 = 5x$$

$$\frac{15}{5} = \frac{5x}{5}$$

$$3 = x$$

The first step of adding $5x$ to both sides of the equation didn't help us isolate x. It just moved the term $5x$ from one side of the equation to the other. Wouldn't a more efficient way of isolating x be to subtract 18 from both sides of the equation first? It would, but we would be left with $-5x$ on the left side of the equation. This does equal ^-5x, so continuing with this approach, the next step is to divide both sides of the equation by $^-5$.

$$18 - 5x = 3$$

$$18 - 5x \underline{- 18} = 3 \underline{- 18}$$

$$\frac{^-5x}{^-5} = \frac{^-15x}{^-5}$$

$$x = 3$$

The advantage of using this second approach is that it takes only two steps instead of three to isolate the variable. The main disadvantage is the risk of "losing" the $-$ sign on the first step when you subtract 18 from both sides of the equation.

When you isolate the variable, you have solved the equation because the last line says $x = $ . . ... Keeping the equation balanced while you isolate the variable results in a new equation that has the same solution—an **equivalent equation**. In Example O, the equation $^-5x = {}^-15$ is equivalent to the original equation, and the equation $x = 3$ is equivalent to $^-5x = {}^-15$.

What can you do if an equation has more than one variable in it?

Example P. The equation $2x + 4y = 12$ has two variables in it.

You can still solve this equation for x (isolate x). Subtract $4y$ from both sides of the equation. Divide each term on both sides of the equation by 2, resulting in the fourth line. Simplify by reducing or evaluating (line 5). Reverse the order of terms on the right side of the equation (line 6).

$$2x + 4y = 12$$

$$2x + 4y \underline{- 4y} = 12 \underline{- 4y}$$

$$2x = 12 - 4y$$

$$\frac{2x}{2} = \frac{12}{2} - \frac{4y}{2}$$

$$x = 6 - 2y$$

$$x = {}^-2y + 6$$

$$x = 6 + {}^-2y$$

Or, you can solve the same equation for y (isolate y). Subtract $2x$ from both sides of the equation, resulting in the third line. Divide each term on both sides of the equation by 4 (line 4). Recognize that $\frac{1x}{2}$ is the same quantity as $\frac{1}{2}x$ (line 6), and reverse the order of terms on the right side of the equation (line 7).

$$2x + 4y = 12$$

$$2x + 4y \underline{- 2x} = 12 \underline{- 2x}$$

$$4y = 12 - 2x$$

$$\frac{4y}{4} = \frac{12}{4} - \frac{2x}{4}$$

$$y = 3 - \frac{1x}{2}$$

$$y = 3 - \frac{1}{2}x$$

$$y = 3 + {}^-\frac{1}{2}x$$

$$y = {}^-\frac{1}{2}x + 3$$

In both cases, the steps follow the reverse order of operations described earlier.

Practice Solving Equations

Solve each equation for x.

1. $x - 13 = 0$　　　　2. $5x = 35$　　　　3. $\frac{x}{4} = 6$

4. $3x - 7 = 5$　　　　5. $5x + 1 = 16$　　　6. $2 + 5x = 12$

7. $6 - 3x = {}^{-}3$　　　8. $4x + 8 = 2x$　　　9. $x + y = 5$

10. $4x - 3y = 12$　　　11. $\frac{2x}{3} + 1 = 15$　　12. $\frac{x}{2} + y = 7$

Solving Inequalities

An inequality is also a math sentence. Instead of "equals" ($=$) inequalities involve "less than" ($<$) or "greater than" ($>$). (Remember that the arrow-head always points to the smaller number.) The main difference between equations and inequalities is that inequalities have an infinite number of solutions, while equations only have one.[1]

Let's look at an inequality that has been solved. An example of a solution statement is $x < 4$. A solution to an inequality is defined in the same way as it is for an equation: any number which, when substituted for x, results in a true statement. So, the number 3 is a solution, and the number 2 is a solution. In fact, any number less than 4 is a solution, including numbers such as 3.9, 3.999, and so forth.

Now look at an inequality that involves one operation: $x + 7 > 9$. This can be solved using the same method as for solving an equation. Isolate the variable and do the same thing to both sides. In this example, if you subtract 7 from both sides of the inequality, you get $x > 2$.

$$x + 7 > 9$$

$$x + 7 \underline{- 7} > 9 \underline{- 7}$$

$$x > 2$$

The only thing that you have to do differently when solving an inequality is when you divide both sides of the equation by a negative number. For example, to solve the inequality ${}^{-}5x < 10$, divide both sides of the inequality by ${}^{-}5$. Since ${}^{-}5$ is a negative number, you have to *reverse* the direction of the inequality. The steps would look like this:

$$^{-}5x < 10$$

$$\frac{^{-}5x}{^{-}5} > \frac{10}{^{-}5}$$

$$x > {}^{-}2$$

---

[1] Equations and inequalities both can have either an infinite number of solutions or no solutions at all. The TABE does not consider these types of math sentences.

It is easy to see why the direction of an inequality is reversed when you divide by a negative number. The inequality $1 < 2$ is true. If you divide both sides of this equality by $^-1$, the left side becomes $^-1$ and the right side becomes $^-2$, and $^-1 > ^-2$. So to preserve truth, you have to change $<$ to $>$.

Don't be fooled by an inequality such as $3x < ^-6$. To solve this, you have to divide both sides of the inequality by 3. The fact that the right side of the inequality is a negative number does *not* mean you should change the direction of the inequality. Whether you change the direction of the inequality depends on the number you are dividing (or multiplying) both sides by.

Inequalities can also be of the form $\leq$ (less than or equal to) or $\geq$ (greater than or equal to). As an example, look at the statement $x \leq 9$. The number 9 is a solution to this inequality because 9 is less than or equal to 9. But the number 9 is *not* a solution to the inequality $x < 9$ because 9 is not less than 9.

A few more examples to illustrate these ideas follow.

Example Q. Solve $2x + 5 > 7$.

First subtract 5 from both sides. Then divide both sides by 2.

$$2x + 5 > 7$$
$$2x + 5 - 5 > 7 - 5$$
$$2x > 2$$
$$\frac{2x}{2} > \frac{2}{2}$$
$$x > 1$$

Example R. Solve $\frac{x}{4} < 5$.

Multiply both sides by 4.

$$\frac{x}{4} < 5$$
$$4 \times \frac{x}{4} < 4 \times 5$$
$$x < 20$$

Example S. Solve $^-3x - 4 > 8$.

Add 4 to both sides of the inequality. Then divide both sides of the inequality by $^-3$. Change the direction of the inequality because you divided by a negative number ($^-3$).

$$^-3x - 4 > 8$$
$$^-3x - 4 + 4 > 8 + 4$$
$$^-3x > 12$$
$$\frac{^-3x}{^-3} < \frac{12}{^-3}$$
$$x < ^-4$$

Example T. Solve $5 - x < 1$.

Subtract 5 from both sides of the inequality. This leaves $-x$ on the left side and –4 on the right side. But $-x$ is the same quantity as $^{-}1x$, so divide both sides of the inequality by $^{-}1$.

$$5 - x < 1$$
$$\underline{5 - 5} - x < \underline{1 - 5}$$
$$^{-}1x < {}^{-}4$$
$$x > 4$$

Another method to solve this problem is to first add x to both sides of the inequality. Then subtract 1 from both sides.

$$5 - x < 1$$
$$5 - x \underline{+ x} < 1 \underline{+ x}$$
$$5 < 1 + x$$
$$5 \underline{- 1} < 1 + x \underline{- 1}$$
$$4 < x$$
$$x > 4$$

If you use this method, you don't have to remember to change the direction of the inequality or to work with negative numbers.

Practice Solving Inequalities

Solve each inequality for x.

1. $x - 5 < 7$ 2. $2x + 4 > 2$ 3. $\frac{x}{3} \leq -5$ 4. $4 - 3x \geq 10$

5. $10x \leq 5$ 6. $^{-}x \geq {}^{-}4$ 7. $5x - 7 < 18$ 8. $8 - 3x \leq 5$

PROBLEM SOLVING

Problem solving is about getting answers to "word problems" or "story problems." To do this successfully, you have to read a problem to determine what you must find and what information the problem tells you. These kinds of problems range from very easy to quite difficult, and there is no way to cover every type of problem that you may see. This lesson describes several popular types of "word problems."

1. Markup and discount in retail sales (percent)
2. Tipping in restaurants (percent)
3. Problems involving proportion
4. Fuel efficiency and travel (rates)

Markup and Discount in Retail Sales

Markup in retail sales provides a backdrop for one group of word problems involving percents. An item has a regular retail price. This price reflects a percent markup from the wholesale price to the dealer. A problem might tell you the percent markup and the retail price, and ask you to find the wholesale price. Or, it may tell you the wholesale price and the percent markup, and ask you to find the retail price. Finally, the problem may tell you the wholesale and retail prices, and you have to find the percent markup. There are three numbers in each of these problems. The problem tells you two of them and asks you to find the third.

Example A. The wholesale price of a leather jacket is $150. It is marked up 60%. What is the retail price? This problem tells you the wholesale price and the percent markup. You have to find the retail price.

The retail price is $150 plus 60% of $150. Just focus on 60% of $150. Using the language of Lesson 4, 150 is the whole, and 60 is the percent. You have to find the part. The formula is *Part* = % × *Whole* ÷ 100. Substituting the values for this problem, *Part* = 60 × 150 ÷ 100 = 90. So the markup is $90. Add this to the $150 wholesale price, and the retail price is $240.

There is a **shortcut** for this problem. First recall that 60% = 0.6. The retail price is 1 × wholesale price + 0.6 × wholesale price. This equals

1.6 × wholesale price (see the Distributive Property of Multiplication over Addition in Lesson 6). So the retail price is just 1.6 × 150 = 240.

- To find the retail price, change the percent markup to a decimal, add it to 1, and multiply the result by the wholesale price.

Example B. The wholesale price of a necklace is $250 and its retail price is $425. What is the percent markup?

First subtract $250 from $425 to find the *amount* of the markup, $175. Again in the language of Lesson 4, the part is 175 and the whole is 250. You want to find the percent. The formula is *% = Part ÷ Whole × 100*. Substituting the numbers for this problem, % = 175 ÷ 250 × 100 = 70. The percent markup of the necklace is 70%.

There is a **shortcut** for this problem as well. Divide the retail price by the wholesale price: 425 ÷ 250 = 1.7. This result, 1.7, is the wholesale price plus 70% of the wholesale price.

- To find the percent markup, divide the retail price by the wholesale price, and subtract 1. Move the decimal point of the answer two places to the right.

Example C. A high-definition television set you want retails for $2300. You learn that this price is the result of a 30% markup over the wholesale price. What is the wholesale price?

Call the wholesale price *w*. Using the shortcut from the last example, 1.3*w* = 2300. Solve this equation for *w*.

$$1.3w = 2300$$
$$\frac{1.3w}{1.3} = \frac{2300}{1.3}$$
$$w = 1769.23$$

The wholesale price is $1769.23.

This problem also has a shortcut. Change the 30% markup to a decimal and add it to 1 to get 1.3. Then divide $2300 by 1.3 to get the wholesale price: $2300 ÷ 1.3 = $1769.23.

- To find the wholesale price, change the percent markup to a decimal and add it to 1. Then divide the retail price by the answer.

Discount (sales) provides another group of problems in retail. The three variations of discounting problems correspond exactly to the preceding three wholesale-retail variations. The retail price of an item and the % discount are given. You have to find the discounted (sale) price. Or, the retail price and sale price are given, and you have to find the % discounted. Finally, the sale price and the % discount are given, and you have to find the retail price.

Both markup and discount problems involve three numbers, of which two are given and one must be found. The difference between the two types of problems is the quantity that represents the "whole" in the percent scenario. When looking at percent markup, the wholesale (lower) price is the whole on which the percent is calculated. In the discount problems, the retail (higher) price is the whole on which percent is calculated.

These differences can be illustrated by an example. Suppose you have an item that retails for $100. A 25% discount on that item results in a $75 sale price. If you then raise this $75 price by 25%, the new price would only be $93.75 instead of the $100. This is because 25% was based on 100 for the reduction, but it was based on 75 for the increase.

Example D. The retail price of a computer game is $57. A store has the game on sale at 15% off. What is the sale price?

This problem tells you the retail price and the % discount and asks you for the discounted price. In the language of percents, 57 is the whole and 15 is the percent. You must find the part (discount) and subtract it from the whole. The formula is *Part* = % × *Whole* ÷ 100. Substitute the number from this problem to get *Part* = 15 × 57 ÷ 100 = 8.55. So the discount $8.55 is subtracted from $57 resulting in a sale price of $48.45.

There is a **shortcut** for this problem. If there is a 15% discount, you actually pay 85% (100% − 15%). So the discounted price is 0.85 × $57 = $48.45.

- To find the discounted price, subtract the percent discount from 100, move the decimal two places to the left, and multiply by the original price.

Example E. George buys a $15 calculator for $12. What is the percent discount?

The amount of the discount is $3. This is the part. The retail price is $15. This is the whole. % = *Part* ÷ *Whole* × 100, so % = 3 ÷ 15 × 100 = 20. A 20% savings was realized.

- To find the % discount, divide the discounted price by the regular price and move the decimal two places to the right.

Example F. Sue bought a pair of jeans for $40 at a sale where all merchandise is 30% off. What was the original price?

Using the idea from the previous example, the $40 sale price is 70% (100% − 30%) of the original price. Divide 40 by 0.7 to get the original price of $57.14.

- To find the original price, subtract the percent discount from 100 and move the decimal two places left. Divide the sale price by the answer.

These six examples don't cover every type of percent problem. Instead of asking how much was paid for an item after a discount, a question could ask how much the discount was or how much was saved. Or instead of asking for the retail price of an item after a percent markup, a problem might ask what the markup is. You need to be sure to read a problem carefully to ensure that you answer the question asked.

Tipping in a Restaurant

When you eat in a restaurant, you usually leave a tip. It is customary to leave an amount that is between 15% and 20% of the bill (less tax). A problem might tell you the amount of a bill and ask the amount of a tip of 15%. Or, a problem might tell you the amount of the bill, the amount left as a tip, and ask what percent the tip is. Finally, a problem might tell you the total amount that was left for the bill and the tip, tell you the percent of the bill that is the tip, and ask how much the tip is.

Example G. The Johnson family went to dinner, and the bill was $52.50 without tax. The service was excellent, so Ms. Johnson left a 20% tip. How much money was this?

You need to calculate 20% of $52.50. In the language of percents (Lesson 4), the tip is the part and the amount of the bill is the whole. The formula is *Part* = % × *Whole* ÷ 100. Substitute the numbers for this problem to get *Part* = 20 × 52.5 ÷ 100 = 10.5. Ms. Johnson should leave a $10.50 tip.

There is a nice **shortcut** for this problem in case you don't happen to have a calculator with you in the restaurant. The decimal equivalent of 10% is 0.1. When you multiply a number by 0.1, move the decimal point one place to the left (see Lesson 1). So 10% of $52.50 is $5.25. Since 20% is double 10%, a 20% tip is double $5.25, or $10.50. For a 15% tip, you would add half of $5.25 (about $2.60) to $5.25 for an amount of $7.85.

Example H. Six friends went to lunch at a nice restaurant. The bill, without tax, was $65 and they decided to leave $2 each as a tip. What percent tip did they leave?

Since six people each left $2, the total tip was $12. In this problem, 12 is the part, and 65 is the total. You must find the percent. The formula is % = *Part* ÷ *Whole* × 100. Substituting, you get % = 12 ÷ 65 × 100 = 18.5, approximately. The group left an 18.5% tip.

Example I. Jim took Mary out for a business lunch. Jim remembered that the cost of lunch and the tip was $48, but he forgot the cost of the lunch. He always leaves a 20% tip. How much was the tip?

You can use the same strategy as described in the shortcut of Example A to solve this problem. The $48 is 1.2 times the cost of the lunch. Suppose

c stands for the cost of lunch. Then $1.2c = 48$. To solve this equation for c, divide both sides of the equation by 1.2.

$$1.2c = 48$$
$$\frac{1.2c}{1.2} = \frac{48}{1.2}$$
$$c = 40$$

The cost of the lunch is $40. Subtract $40 from $48 to get $8 for the tip.

Problems Involving Proportion

A proportion says that two fractions are equal. For example, $\frac{3}{8} = \frac{15}{40}$ is a proportion. You encounter proportions all the time in your daily life. This proportion could mean that if 3 notebooks cost $8, then you would expect 15 notebooks to cost $40. Or, it might mean that if you get 3 hits in 8 at bats in baseball, you would expect to get 15 hits in 40 at bats. Or, it could mean that if 3 of 8 people have brown hair, you would expect 15 of 40 people to have brown hair.

Every proportion has four numbers. In a proportion problem, you know three of the numbers, and you have to find the fourth.

Example J. In his first game of the season, Michael made 6 of 7 free throws. If he takes 182 free throws during the whole season, how many would he expect to make at this rate?

Set up the proportion $\frac{6}{7} = \frac{x}{182}$. To solve a proportion, you multiply the two numbers that are diagonally across from each other. In this case, $7x = 6 \times 182$. Then divide by the number diagonally across from x.[1] So $x = 6 \times 182 \div 7 = 156$. Michael can expect to make 156 free throws.

Example K. A certain recipe calls for $\frac{1}{4}$ cup of sugar to make enough for 6 people. Amanda has invited 15 guests for dinner and wants to use this recipe. How much sugar will she need to use?

Set up the proportion $\frac{1/4}{6} = \frac{x}{15}$ and solve for x:

$$x = \frac{1}{4} \times 15 \div 6 = \frac{1}{4} \times \frac{\overset{5}{\cancel{15}}}{1} \times \frac{1}{\underset{2}{\cancel{6}}} = \frac{5}{8}$$

Travel and Fuel Efficiency

Two other useful types of word problems arise when you drive. One is fuel efficiency. In the United States, fuel efficiency is measured in miles per gallon—how far you can travel on one gallon of fuel. For example, if you can travel

---

[1] This is exactly what you would do if you were to solve this equation using algebra.

380 miles on 20 gallons of fuel, your fuel efficiency is $\frac{380}{20} = 19$ miles per gallon. This is actually just a special type of proportion. If you can travel 380 miles on 20 gallons, how many miles can you travel on 1 gallon: $\frac{380}{20} = \frac{x}{1}$. If you solve this proportion as described earlier, you would get the same 19 miles per gallon answer.

Example L. Raphael's car gets 31 miles per gallon, and his fuel tank holds 12.3 gallons. Can he make a 350-mile trip on one tank of fuel?

Each gallon of fuel is good for 31 miles, so 12.3 gallons of fuel is good for $12.3 \times 31 = 381.3$ miles. So yes, he can make a 350-mile trip on one tank.

A second type of problem involving driving relates the three quantities distance, time, and speed. Let d stand for distance, r for average speed, and t for time. There are three forms of the formula that relate these three quantities:

1. Distance = average speed × time ($d = rt$)

2. Average speed = distance ÷ time ($r = \frac{d}{t}$)

3. Time = distance ÷ average speed ($t = \frac{d}{r}$)

Example M. Pat drives an average of 40 miles per hour for 45 minutes. How far does she travel?

You have to find the distance. Forty-five minutes is $\frac{3}{4}$ hour, so $d = \frac{3}{4} \times 40 = 30$. Pat drives a distance of 30 miles.

Example N. George drives a distance of 325 miles in 6 hours and 30 minutes. Find his average speed.

Six hours and 30 minutes is 6.5 hours, so $r = \frac{325}{6.5} = 50$. George's average speed is 50 miles per hour.

• 60 miles per hour is 1 mile per minute.

Example O. Bob must drive his truck to Columbus by 6:00 P.M. He is now in Cleveland, 142 miles away, and it's 3:30. How fast must he drive (average speed)?

Bob has 2.5 hours to make the trip, and $r = \frac{d}{t} = \frac{142}{2.5}$. Bob must drive an average speed of 56.8 miles per hour.

Other types of word problems—those involving algebra—are discussed in Lesson 8. In those problems you need to formulate an equation that represents relationships among the pieces of information given in the problem.

Practice Problem Solving

1. Bob and his friends have lunch at the golf course, and the bill, excluding tax, amounts to $34. Since they had counter service in a casual atmosphere, they decide to leave a 15% tip. How big a tip should they leave?

2. The price of a used textbook is $36. This is 25% less than a new textbook would cost. How much would a new textbook cost?

3. Deb makes jewelry and sells it to stores who then sell it to customers. She sold one item for $125, and the store marked the price at $200. What is the percent markup?

4. Phil bought a new power drill for 20% off the retail price of $62. How much did he pay for it?

5. Karen has a 2:30 P.M. appointment in Riverside, 15 miles away. She can average 25 miles per hour driving. By what time must she leave, barring any delays, in order to get to her appointment on time?

6. Kenny knows that he averages 28 miles per gallon on his car, and his car has an 18-gallon fuel tank. Can Kenny make a 450-mile trip on one tank?

7. J.J. made 19 of 20 free throws in a basketball game. At this rate, how many of 400 free throws could he expect to make during the season?

8. A $35 shirt is on sale for $28. What is the percent discount?

9. Sam was able to drive his pickup truck 90 miles on 5.6 gallons of gas. Ellen drove her car 130 miles on 6.1 gallons. To the nearest tenth of a gallon, how much better was Ellen's gas mileage than Sam's?

10. Peter bought shares of a certain stock for $12 per share. He sold 50 shares a year later for $800. By what percent did the cost per share go up or down?

APPLIED ALGEBRA

Patterns

People have observed patterns throughout history. There are many patterns in nature. Early astronomers say daylight hours get longer and shorter over time. People who live near the ocean notice the tides ebb and flow. Vegetation grows thick and seemingly dies over the seasons. Natural phenomena such as these can be described, or modeled, using number patterns or picture patterns.

Number Patterns

A number pattern is a sequence of numbers that follows a certain progression. You are generally given the first several numbers of the sequence, and you have to figure out how each number is obtained from its predecessors and use this to obtain the next number in the sequence. This type of problem can range from very simple to quite difficult. Several examples are explained next.

Example A. Find the next number in the sequence 1, 4, 7, 10, ...

Add 3 to each number to get the next number. Another way of looking at this is if you subtract each number from the next one, you always get 3 as the answer. So the next number is 13.

Example B. Find the next number in the sequence 2, 4, 8, 16, 32, ...

Multiply each number by 2 to get the next number. Another way of looking at this is if you divide each number by the one before it, you get 2. So the next number is 64.

Example C. Find the next number in the sequence 1, 2, 5, 14, 41, ...

This problem is much more difficult than the first two examples, and it is a combination of the two. Multiply each number by 3 and subtract 1 to get the next number:

$$3 \times 1 - 1 = 2$$
$$3 \times 2 - 1 = 5$$
$$3 \times 5 - 1 = 14$$
$$3 \times 14 - 1 = 41$$

Following this pattern, the next number is $3 \times 41 - 1 = 122$. Another way to see this pattern is to subtract each number from the next:

$$2 - 1 = 1$$
$$5 - 2 = 3$$
$$14 - 5 = 9$$
$$41 - 14 = 27$$

These differences are increasing powers of 3: $1 = 3^0$, $3 = 3^1$, $9 = 3^2$, $27 = 3^3$, and so forth. So the next number should be $3^4 = 81$ more than 41, or $41 + 81 = 122$.

Example D.   Find the next number in the sequence 1, 1, 2, 3, 5, 8, 13, 21, ...

This is called the Fibonacci sequence, made famous in the book, *The DaVinci Code*. After the first two 1s, you get each number by adding the two that precede it:

$$1 + 1 = 2$$
$$2 + 1 = 3$$
$$3 + 2 = 5$$
$$5 + 3 = 8$$
$$8 + 5 = 13$$
$$13 + 8 = 21$$

So the next number in the sequence is $13 + 21 = 34$.

Figuring out number patterns is not always easy. It takes practice. If you have trouble with these, be sure to read the explanations that go with the practice problems.

Picture Patterns

Picture patterns are exactly what they sound like. You are given a sequence of pictures, and you have to determine what the next picture looks like.

Example E.   Determine the next picture in the sequence:

Each picture is a square with one more dot on each side. So the next picture is

Example F. Determine the next picture in the sequence:

There are three different pictures, and then they repeat. So the 8th picture is just like the 5th and the 2nd:

Practice Pattern

Find the next number in each sequence.

1. 1, 4, 7, 10, 13, . . .

2. 11, 6, 1, ⁻4, ⁻9, . . .

3. 1, 2, 4, 7, 11, 16, . . .

4. ⁻8, 7 , ⁻6, 5, ⁻4, 3, . . .

5. 1, ⁻2, ⁻5, ⁻8, ⁻11, . . .

6. 2, 5, 10, 17, 26, . . .

7. ⁻7, ⁻5, ⁻1, 5, 13, . . .

Find the missing number in the sequence.

8. 2, 7, 12, 17, —, 27, 32, . . .

9. 2, 6, 18, —, 162, 846, . . .

10. 6, 5, 3, 0, —, ⁻9, ⁻15, . . .

Sketch the next picture in the sequence.

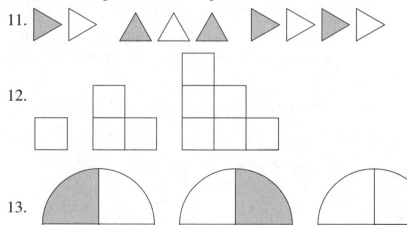

11.

12.

13.

Formulas

Formulas provide a way of capturing the essence of a pattern by using algebra. A **formula** is a mathematical equation that tells you how to find one quantity when you know other quantities. You will see several geometry formulas in the next lesson. These are used to find the perimeters, areas, and volumes of geometric figures from other measurements. There are lots of formulas in science and other quantitative fields such as economics.

There are also formulas that reflect specific circumstances. For example, suppose you want to rent a canoe for an afternoon of leisure. The rental company charges you a $10 fee plus $8 per hour of use. If t stands for the length of time you rent the canoe, the formula for the rental cost C for t hours is $C = 10 + 8t$.

Example G. You are on vacation in Paris and it feels very warm out. A sign on a bank shows that the temperature is 30° Celsius. You want to know what this is in Fahrenheit.

The formula for converting Celsius temperature C to Fahrenheit temperature F is $F = \frac{9}{5}C + 32$. Substitute 30 for C and do the calculations:

$$F = \frac{9}{5} \times 30 + 32$$

$$F = \frac{9}{{}_1\cancel{5}} \times \cancel{30}^6 + 32$$

$$F = 9 \times 6 + 32$$
$$F = 86$$

The Fahrenheit temperature is 86°.

You've seen the formula $d = rt$ in Lesson 7. This formula says that the distance an object (such as an automobile) travels is equal to the average speed times the amount of time it travels. You may need to use algebra to solve a formula problem.

Example H. Suppose you need to drive 300 miles, and you know you can make that drive at an average speed of 45 miles per hour. How long will it take?

Use the formula $d = rt$, and substitute 300 for d and 45 for r:

$$300 = 45t$$

$$\frac{300}{45} = \frac{\cancel{45}^1 t}{{}_1\cancel{45}}$$

$$6\frac{2}{3} = t$$

The trip will take 6 hours and 40 minutes ($\frac{2}{3}$ hour).

When you put your money into a savings account, it earns interest. Banks will tell you the interest rate you will earn. This is the amount by which your money will grow over time. The formula that applies is $A = P(1 + i)$, where i is the annual interest rate expressed as a %, P is the amount you put into the account, and A is the amount in your account a year later.

Example I. You put $500 into a savings account that earns 2% interest a year. How much is in your account after 1 year?

Use the formula $A = P(1 + i)$, with $P = 500$ and $i = .02$ (2% must be changed to a decimal for use in this formula):

$$A = 500(1 + .02)$$
$$A = 500(1.02)$$
$$A = 510$$

There is $510 in your savings account after 1 year. If you subtract the amount you started with, you get the amount of interest earned: $510 − $500 = $10.

Practice Formula

1. To change centimeters to inches, use the formula *inches* = 2.54 × *centimeters*. How many centimeters are there in a foot?

2. To change Fahrenheit temperature to Celsius temperature, use the formula $C = \frac{5}{9}(F - 32)$. What is the Celsius temperature of 150°F?

3. The simple interest formula is $A = P(1 + r)^t$, where r is the annual interest rate (in decimal form), P is the amount you invest, and A is the amount your investment is worth after t years. How much is $100 worth after 10 years if the interest rate is 3%?

4. Stuart drives an average of 36 miles per hour for 4 hours and 15 minutes. How far does he travel?

5. Kathy has to drive to Phoenix, which is 350 miles away. Her gas tank holds 15 gallons, and her car gets 22 miles per gallon. Can she make it to Phoenix on one tank?

6. The density of a substance is given by the formula $d = \frac{m}{v}$, where d is density, m is mass in grams, and v is volume in cubic centimeters. What is the density of gold if 2 cubic centimeters has a mass of 38.6 grams?

7. The intensity of light in lumens at a distance of x feet from a 100-watt light bulb is given by the formula $I = \frac{100}{x^2}$. What is the intensity of light 5 feet from such a bulb?

Words to Symbols

Students often say that "word problems" or "story problems" are the most dreaded types of algebra problems. To be successful at these types of problems, you must (a) be sure to read the problem carefully enough to understand what it's asking you for and (b) be skilled at translating words into math symbols. This part of the lesson is about (b). Let's start with the symbols $>$, $\geq$, $<$, and $\leq$.

1. $>$ means "greater than" or "larger than."

   $6 > 5$ means "6 is greater than 5."

   $x > 3$ means "a number is more than 3."

2. $\geq$ means "greater than or equal to" or "not less than" or "at least."

   $6 \geq 5$ means "6 is greater than or equal to 5."

   $x \geq 3$ means "a number is not less than 3."

   $x \geq 21$ means "a number is at least 21."

3. $<$ means "less than" or "smaller than."

   $5 < 6$ means "5 is less than 6."

   $x < 2$ means "a number is less than 2."

4. $\leq$ means "less than or equal to" or "not larger than" or "at most."

   $6 \leq 6$ means "6 is less than or equal to 6."

   $x \leq 25$ means "a number is not more than 25."

   $x \leq 10$ means "number is at most 10."

In several of the preceding examples, x stands for a number. In the examples that follow, the phrase "Let __ stand for a number," is used. This phrase **defines a variable**.

Example J. Translate "I have more than 100 baseball cards in my collection."

Let b stand for the number of baseball cards in my collection: $b > 100$.

Example K. Translate "You have to be at least 18 years of age to vote."

Let a stand for your age in years: $a \geq 18$.

Example L. Translate "The nightclub's capacity is 250 people."

Let c stand for the capacity of the nightclub: $c \leq 250$.

Example M. Translate "I weigh less than 150 pounds."

Let w stand for my weight in pounds: $w < 150$.

Other phrases frequently need to be translated. Phrases in English translate to expressions in math.

1. Five more than a number: $x + 5$ or $5 + x$
2. Five less than a number: $x - 5$
3. Three times a number: $3x$
4. One-third of a number $\frac{1}{3}x$ or $\frac{x}{3}$

Now let's look at some examples that combine several phrases.

Example N. Write an equation or inequality for "Eight less than 5 times a number is 30."

Let x stand for the number. Five times x is $5x$. Eight less than this is $5x - 8$. This gives you the equation $5x - 8 = 30$. The phrase "less than" in this problem tells you to subtract. It does *not* mean $<$.

Example O. Write an equation or an inequality for "Two more than half a number is more than six."

Let x stand for the number. Half of x is $\frac{x}{2}$. Two more than this is $\frac{x}{2} + 2$. This gives you the inequality $\frac{x}{2} + 2 > 6$.

Example P. Write an equation or an inequality for "The sum of 3 and negative six times a number is at least 200."

Let x stand for the number. Negative six times x is ^-6x. A sum results from adding, so the sum of 3 and $^-6$ times a number is $^-6x + 3$. The phrase "at least 200" means 200 or more. This gives you the inequality $^-6x + 3 \geq 200$.

Still other combination problems require you to use parentheses. Look at the phrase "five times one more than a number." If you let x stand for the number, one more than x is $x + 1$. Five times this quantity is $5(x + 1)$. The expression $5x + 1$ means one more than five times a number. You get a different answer adding 1 to a number first and then multiplying by 5 than you'd get multiplying the number by 5 and then adding 1. For example, if x were 4, then

$$5(x + 1) = 5(\underline{4} + 1) = 5(5) = 25, \text{ but}$$

$$5x + 1 = 5(\underline{4}) + 1 = 20 + 1 = 21$$

Practice Words to Symbols

In each of the following problems, let x stand for a number. Write an expression, equation, or inequality for each.

1. Ten more than a number.
2. Ten is more than a number.

3. Eight less than 12 times a number.

4. Three times 5 more than a number.

5. Three times a number is less than 9.

6. Two less than 6 times a number is equal to 25.

7. Two times 5 more than a number is greater than 50.

8. Ten less than 3 times a number is at least 15.

9. Four less than a number is less than four.

10. Seven times 5 more than a number is at most 50.

GEOMETRY

Geometry is the study of shapes. The geometry of flat surfaces (two dimensions) is called **plane geometry**. **Solid geometry** is about three-dimensional figures, such as boxes, cylinders, cones, and pyramids.

You see geometry all around you. A yield sign is a triangle. A stop sign is an octagon. The U.S. Department of Defense building in Washington is in the shape of a pentagon. The curbs of a street are parallel lines. The letter T consists of perpendicular lines. Common three-dimensional figures are cereal boxes, water glasses, and ice cream cones. The great pyramids of Egypt are probably the best-known examples of that shape.

Much of the geometry you need to know for the TABE A is definitions of various figures and relationships between them. You must also know what certain symbols mean. In other problems, you must recognize geometry patterns. Finally, you will have to apply a few geometry facts to solve some problems. First you need to review a long list of definitions.

Definitions

Line: a straight line that extends forever in both directions. Line AB ($\overleftrightarrow{AB}$) is shown.

Line segment: a line that stops at **both** ends. Segment AB ($\overline{AB}$) is shown.

Ray: a line with **one** endpoint. Ray AB ($\overrightarrow{AB}$) is shown.

Parallel lines: a pair of lines (or line segments or rays) that never cross each other, like railroad tracks.

Perpendicular lines: a pair of lines (or line segments or rays) that form a right angle (90°), like the corner of a piece of paper.

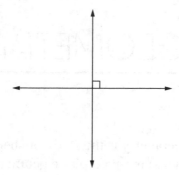

Angle: Two rays with the same endpoint. This common endpoint is called the **vertex** of the angle. The rays themselves are called the **sides** of the angle. Angle A ($\angle A$) is shown.

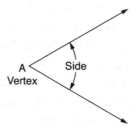

Look at the following figure. There are three angles with vertex A. You could not just call this $\angle A$ because you couldn't be sure which angle had that name. You need three letters to name the angle. The middle letter is the vertex, and the other two letters are on the sides. $\angle BAC$ is drawn with a heavier line.

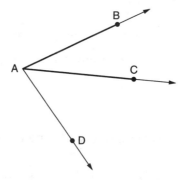

Right angle: 90°. Perpendicular lines form right angles.

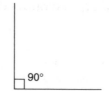

Acute angle: less than 90°.

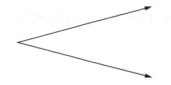

Obtuse angle: more than 90°.

Supplementary angles: two angles that add up to 180°.

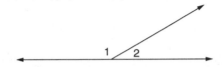

Complementary angles: two angles that add up to 90°.

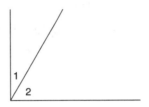

Transversal: a line that cuts across two other lines in different places.

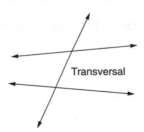

A **polygon** is a geometric shape made of line segments attached end-to-end. The segments are called the **sides** of the polygon. The endpoints of the sides are called the **vertices** (plural of the word "vertex"). A polygon is called a **regular polygon** if all the sides are equal in length. A regular octagon (eight-sided polygon) is shown next to illustrate these parts.

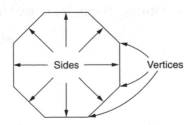

The simplest polygon (smallest number of sides) is a **triangle**. A triangle can be classified according to its sides.

- **Isosceles triangle:** Two sides of equal length.

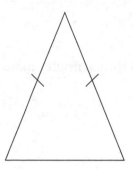

- **Equilateral triangle:** all three sides have equal length.

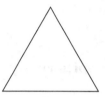

- **Scalene triangle:** all three sides have different lengths.

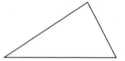

A triangle can also be classified according to its angles.

- **Right triangle:** one right angle.

- **Acute triangle:** all three angles are acute (less than 90°).

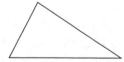

- **Obtuse triangle:** one obtuse angle (more than 90°).

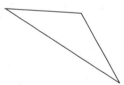

Both angles and sides can be used to classify a triangle. For example, an **isosceles right triangle** is shown next.

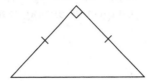

Quadrilaterals are polygons with four sides. The diagonals of a quadrilateral are segments that connect opposite vertices. Types of quadrilaterals and their properties are listed next.

- **Square**
  - Two pairs of parallel sides.
  - Four equal sides.
  - Four right angles.
  - Equal diagonals.

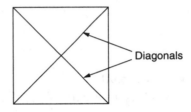

Diagonals

- **Rectangle**
  - Two pairs of parallel sides.
  - Two pairs of equal sides.
  - Four right angles.
  - Equal diagonals.

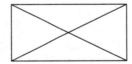

- **Parallelogram**
  - Two pairs of parallel sides.
  - Opposite angles equal.
  - Diagonals bisect each other (cut each other in half).

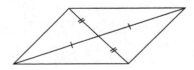

- **Rhombus**
  - Four equal sides.
  - Opposite angles equal.
  - Diagonals are perpendicular.

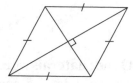

- **Kite**
  - Two pairs of equal consecutive sides.
  - Diagonals are perpendicular.
  - One diagonal bisects the other.

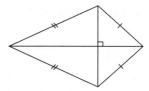

- **Trapezoid**
  - Only one pair of parallel sides.

Other polygons whose names you should know are **hexagon** (six sides) and **octagon** (eight sides). Examples are illustrated next.

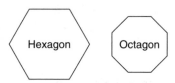

Congruent polygons have the same shape and size. An example of congruent triangles is shown next.

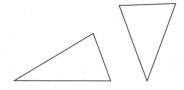

Similar polygons have the same shape but different sizes. Similar polygons have equal angles but different side lengths. An example of similar pentagons is shown next.

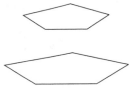

If two polygons are similar, the lengths of their corresponding sides are proportional. For example, suppose you know that the two triangles next ($\triangle ABC$ and $\triangle XYZ$) are similar. What is the length of side $\overline{YZ}$?

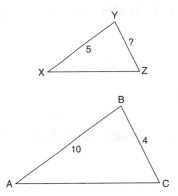

Since $\overline{AB}$ is twice as long as $\overline{XY}$, $\overline{BC}$ must be twice as long as $\overline{YZ}$. This means the length of $\overline{YZ}$ is 2.

A **circle** is defined as a set of points that are equidistant from a given point (center). The **radius** of a circle is the distance that each point on the circle is from its center. The **diameter** is a segment that goes through the center and has its endpoints on the circle.

The **circumference** of a circle is the distance around.

Please be sure to understand that a circle is only the curve you see. Points inside a circle are *not* part of the circle.

A **chord** of a circle is a segment whose endpoints lie on the circle. A **tangent** to a circle is a line, ray, or line segment that just touches the circle at one point. A **secant** to a circle is a line or ray that intersects the circle at two points.

A circle with its related lines, rays, or segments is shown next.

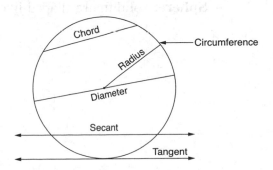

You need to be able to match some **solid figures** with their names.

- **Pyramid:** solid figure with triangular sides that come to a point.

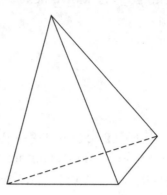

- **Cylinder:** solid figure shaped like a can.

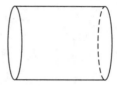

- **Rectangular prism:** solid figure shaped like a box.

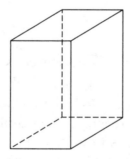

- **Cone:** solid figure shaped like an ice cream cone.

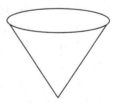

- **Sphere:** solid figure shaped like a ball.

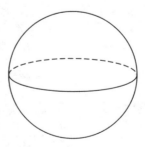

Practice Geometry Definitions

1. Which of these figures are similar?

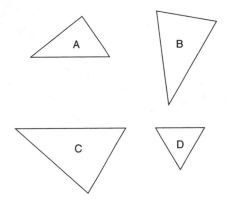

2. Which of these triangles is congruent to the shaded triangle?

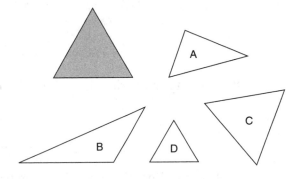

3. Which of these figures is a rhombus?

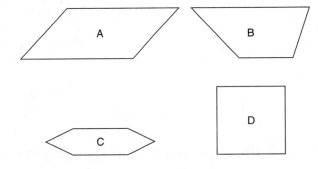

4. Billy is making a cylinder out of cardboard. What combination of shapes does he need to cut out?

5. What is the complement of a 47° angle?

6. What is the supplement of a 55° angle?

7. Which pair of figures is congruent?

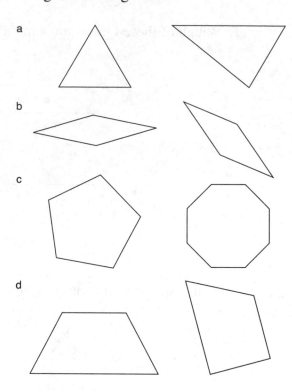

8. What type of triangle is $\triangle ABC$ according to its sides?

9. If the radius of a circle is 20 inches, what is its diameter?

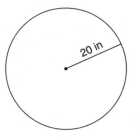

10. What special name is given to the line in the next figure?

Triangle Facts

There are several important facts about triangles.

- The angles of *any* triangle add up to 180°.
- The **base angles** of an isosceles triangle are the ones that are opposite the equal sides. These angles are equal.
- Since the three sides of an equilateral triangle are equal, the three angles are also equal, and each is $180° \div 3 = 60°$. This is shown in the next figure.

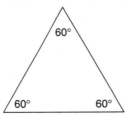

- In a right triangle, two of the sides are sides of the right angle. These are called the **legs** of the right triangle. The third side is opposite the right angle. It is called the **hypotenuse** of the right triangle. Call the lengths of the legs a and b, and call the length of the hypotenuse c. The **Pythagorean Theorem** says that $a^2 + b^2 = c^2$. This fact only applies to *right triangles*. The Pythagorean Theorem is illustrated next.

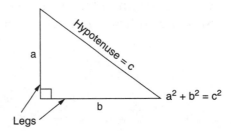

Example A. The legs of a right triangle are 3 feet and 4 feet long. What is the length of the hypotenuse?

In this example $a = 3$ and $b = 4$. According to the Pythagorean Theorem, the square of the hypotenuse $c^2 = 3^2 + 4^2 = 9 + 16 = 25$. The length of the hypotenuse is therefore $\sqrt{25}$, or 5 feet. (See Lesson 5 for a review of square roots.)

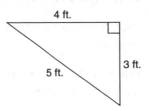

It is also true that if you add the squares of two sides of a triangle and you get the square of the third side, the triangle must be a right triangle. This is called the **converse** of the Pythagorean Theorem.

Example B. Suppose a triangle has sides of length 5 inches, 12 inches, and 13 inches. Is this a right triangle?

$5^2 = 25$, $12^2 = 144$, $13^2 = 169$, and $25 + 144 = 169$, so yes, it is a right triangle.

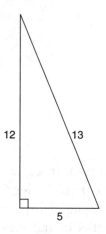

Example C. Suppose one leg of a right triangle is 6 cm, and the hypotenuse is 10 cm. Find the length of the other leg.

Call the length of the other leg b. Then $6^2 + b^2 = 10^2$, or $36 + b^2 = 100$. Subtract 36 from both sides of this equation to find $b^2 = 100 - 36 = 64$. So $b = \sqrt{64} = 8$.

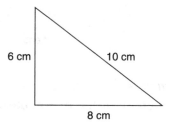

Practice Using Triangle Facts

1. Two angles of a triangle are 50° and 35°. What is the third angle?

2. One base angle of an isosceles triangle is 40°. What are the other two angles?

3. The two legs of a right triangle are 6 meters and 8 meters. What is the length of the hypotenuse?

4. The sides of a triangle are 4 inches, 6 inches, and 8 inches. Is this a right triangle?

5. One leg of a right triangle is 12 feet, and the hypotenuse is 15 feet. What is the length of the other leg?

6. Matt walks 50 feet north and 120 feet east. How far is he from his starting point (in feet)?

7. Two angles of a triangle are 95° and 40°. What type of angle is the third angle?

Perimeter, Area, and Volume

Perimeter, area, and volume are ways of measuring the size of geometrical objects. For example, you measure **area** when you determine how much wall-to-wall carpeting you need for a room or how much wallpaper you need. You measure **perimeter** when determining how much fencing you need around a yard, or how many bricks you need to edge the garden. When you buy mulch for the garden, you must determine the **volume** you need to achieve a certain depth.

Perimeter Formulas

- Square: $P = 4s$

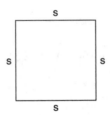

- Rectangle: $P = 2l + 2w$

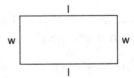

- Triangle: $P = s_1 + s_2 + s_3$

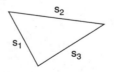

- Circle (called the **circumference**): $C = \pi d$, or $C = 2\pi r$ ($\pi \approx 3.14$)

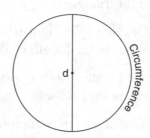

Area Formulas

- Square: $A = s^2$

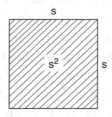

- Rectangle: $A = lw$

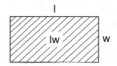

- Triangle: $A = \dfrac{1}{2}bh$

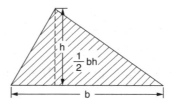

b is any one side of the triangle, and h is the segment from the vertex opposite b and perpendicular to b.

- Circle: πr^2 ($\pi \approx 3.14$)

Volume Formulas

- Cube: $V = s^3$

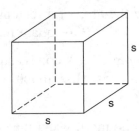

- Rectangular prism: $V = lwh$

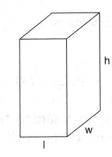

- Cylinder: $V = \pi r^2 h$

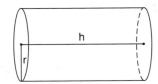

- Cone: $V = \frac{1}{3}\pi r^2 h$

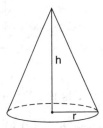

- Sphere: $V = \frac{4}{3}\pi r^3$

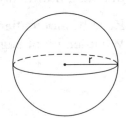

Example D. A rectangular room is 18 feet by 22 feet. What is the area of the room?

Since the area of a rectangle is lengh times width, the area of the room is $18 \times 22 = 396$ square feet.

Example E. A cone-shaped cup has a diameter of 3 inches and a height of 5 inches. How much water, to the nearest tenth of a cubic inch, will it hold?

The amount of water the cup holds is its volume. The formula for a volume of a cone is $V = \frac{1}{3}\pi r^2 h$. For this problem, $r = 1.5$ (half the diameter) and $h = 5$. Therefore $V = \frac{1}{3}(3.14)(1.5)^2(5) \approx 11.8$ cubic inch.

Perimeter, Area, and Volume Practice

1. A box measures 5 feet long, 2 feet wide, and 1 foot high. What is the volume of the box?

The Conti family is planning to clean their swimming pool. The diagram below shows the measurements of the pool. Study the diagram. Then do problems 2–4.

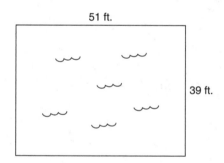

51 ft.

39 ft.

2. What is the length of the pool in yards?

3. If the pool on average is 4 feet deep, how many cubic feet of water will it hold?

4. The garden hose fills the pool at a rate of 240 cubic feet per hour. At this rate, how many hours will it take to fill the pool?

5. Rose has a circular garden in the backyard. It is 15 feet in diameter. What length of edging does she need to enclose the garden?

A rectangular room is 14 feet by 18 feet and has an 8-foot-high ceiling. The walls of the room need to be painted. Use this information to answer questions 7 and 8.

7. What is the total area of the walls?

8. If a gallon of paint covers 200 square feet, how many gallons need to be bought?

9. A soda can has a radius of 4 centimeters and a height of 18 centimeters. What is its volume?

10. Jamesburg High School has a circular track with a diameter of 50 meters. What is the area of the grass inside the circular track?

LESSON 10 | MEASUREMENT

This lesson reviews measurement of time, length, liquid volume, weight, and temperature. There is a universal standard for measuring **time**. There are two sets of measurement units for measuring length, liquid volume, weight, and temperature. The **customary** (English) **system** is the main system of measurement units in the United States. The **metric system** is used in most of the world.

Units of Time

Units of time are somewhat inexact because they have evolved over centuries and are based roughly on movement of the sun and the moon.

1. Second is the basic unit.
2. 60 seconds make 1 minute.
3. 60 minutes make 1 hour.
4. 24 hours make 1 day.
5. 7 days make 1 week.
6. 4 weeks make about a month, which varies in length from 28 to 31 days.
7. 52 weeks make about a year.
8. 12 months make a year.
9. 10 years make a decade.
10. 100 years make a century.

There are also fractions of a second that have important measurement roles in sports, science, and technology:

1. 10 tenths of a second make a second.
2. 100 hundredths of a second make a second.
3. 1000 milliseconds make a second.
4. 1,000,000 nanoseconds make a second.

A summary of the various types of customary and metric units follows.

Units of Length

Customary	Metric
Foot is the basic unit.	Meter is the basic unit.
12 inches make 1 foot.	100 centimeters make 1 meter.
3 feet make 1 yard.	10 millimeters make 1 centimeter.
1760 yards (5280 feet) make 1 mile.	1000 meters make 1 kilometer.

Example A.　Samantha wants to fence in her flower garden, which has a perimeter of 60 feet. Fencing comes in 2-yard sections. How many sections of fencing will she need?

Since there are 3 feet to a yard, 60 feet is 60 ÷ 3 = 20 yards. If each section is 2 yards, Samantha will need 10 sections.

Example B.　Michelle trained for her track meet by running 250 meters, 175 meters, 300 meters, and 275 meters on four consecutive days. How many kilometers did she train on these days altogether?

Add these four numbers on a calculator to get 1000 meters or 1 kilometer.

Example C.　George is reading a map that has a scale of 1 centimeter equals 5 kilometers. The map distance to his destination is 8 centimeters. How far away is his destination?

Each centimeter on the map represents 5 kilometers. A map distance of 8 centimeters represents 8 × 5 = 40 kilometers.

Units of Liquid Volume

Customary	Metric
Gallon is the basic unit.	Liter is the basic unit.
4 quarts make 1 gallon.	100 centiliters make one liter.
2 pints make 1 quart.	10 milliliters make one centiliter.

Example D.　Peter makes 10 quarts of lemonade from concentrate. How many gallons of lemonade is this?

Since there are 4 quarts to a gallon, divide 10 by 4 to get 2.5 gallons of lemonade.

Example E.　Bob and Jack's ice cream costs $3 a pint, and Turkey Farm ice cream costs $5.75 for a half-gallon. Which is less expensive?

Since there are 4 quarts to a gallon, a half-gallon is 2 quarts. There are 2 pints to a quart, so there are 4 pints to 2 quarts, or 4 pints to a half-gallon. Four pints of Bob and Jack's ice cream costs $12, compared with $5.75 for a half-gallon of Turkey Farm. Therefore, Turkey Farm ice cream is less expensive.

Example F. Marge needs to take 3 milliliters of medication every other day. How many centiliters of her medication will she take in 30 days?

Since she takes her medication every other day, Marge will take $15 \times 3 = 45$ milliliters of medication in 30 days. Since there are 10 milliliters to a centiliter, this amounts to 4.5 centiliters.

Units of Weight

Customary	Metric
Pound is the basic unit.	Gram is the basic unit.
16 ounces make 1 pound.	1000 milligrams make 1 gram.
2000 pounds make 1 ton.	1000 grams make 1 kilogram.

Example G. A drug enforcement agent seizes 12 pounds of marijuana, which sells on the street for $175 per ounce. What is the street value?

There are 16 ounces to a pound, so $16 \times 12 = 192$ ounces are recovered. At $175 per ounce, the street value is $33,600.

Example H. The Johnsons want to buy stone to landscape their front yard. They will need to buy 3 tons altogether. Their pickup truck will carry 750 pounds per trip. How many trips will they have to make to carry all the stone home in their pickup truck?

Since there are 2000 pounds per ton, 3 tons is 6000 pounds. Divide 6000 by 750 to get 8 trips.

Units of Temperature

Customary	Metric
Degrees Fahrenheit	Degrees Celsius
Water freezes at 32°F	Water freezes at 0°C
Water boils at 212°F	Water boils at 100°C

Example J. Frank's recipe called for water that was almost boiling. Using a Fahrenheit thermometer, he decided to let the water reach 200°F. How much short of boiling was Frank's water?

The boiling point of water is 212°F. Subtract 200 from 212 to get 12°F short of boiling.

Example K. The formula for changing Celsius temperature to Fahrenheit is $F = \frac{9}{5}C + 32$. If it is 20°C in Paris, what is the Fahrenheit temperature?

Substitute 20 for C in the formula: $\frac{9}{\underset{1}{5}}(\overset{4}{20}) + 32 = 36 + 32 = 68°F$.

1. Jim has 435 minutes left on his cell phone. How many hours (to the nearest hundredth) is this?

2. Don picks $\frac{1}{3}$ acre of blueberries on his farm from 8:00 A.M. to 10:00 A.M. At this rate, what time would he finish the entire acre if he takes an hour for lunch?

3. When Jack woke up this morning, the temperature outside was 6°F below zero. By the time he got to work, it was 13° F above zero. How many degrees F did the temperature rise?

4. The length of a cruise ship is 2460 feet. How many football fields is this if a football field is 100 yards?

5. What is the length of $\overline{BD}$?

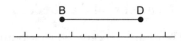

6. A patient in a hospital must receive 20 milliliters of glucose each hour. How many liters of glucose will the patient receive in 12 hours?

7. A chemist needs to add 2.34 kilograms of a substance to a mixture. How many grams of the substance is this?

8. Marylou buys a 50-ounce container of laundry detergent. What is the weight of this detergent in pounds?

9. The temperature in Amsterdam is 20°C. What is this in degrees Fahrenheit? The formula for converting Celsius to Fahrenheit is $F = \frac{9}{5}C + 32$.

10. Suzanne needs 4.25 gallons of paint to paint the first floor of her apartment. How many pints of paint is this?

LESSON 11

COORDINATE GEOMETRY

What Is Coordinate Geometry?

Coordinate geometry uses a **grid** to locate and provide measurements for two-dimensional or one-dimensional figures. The grid—also called a **coordinate plane**—is formed by two number lines placed perpendicular to one another. The horizontal number line is called the **x-axis** and the vertical number line is called the **y-axis**. Parallel horizontal and vertical lines are drawn at the integer values to form the grid. A coordinate plane such as this is illustrated next.

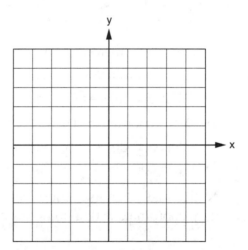

You can locate a point on the grid by its **coordinates**, written as a pair of numbers in parentheses. The first number is the **x-coordinate**, and the second number is the **y-coordinate**. The point where the x-axis and y-axis cross has coordinates $(0, 0)$ and is called the **origin**.

A point is to the right of the origin if the x-coordinate is a positive number and to the left of the origin if it is a negative number. A point is above the origin if its y-coordinate is a positive number and is below the origin if it is a negative number. You plot a point when you put a dot on the grid at the x-coordinate and y-coordinate.

Notice that if both coordinates are positive, a point is in the upper right of the grid. This is called Quadrant I. Quadrant II is the upper-left portion of the grid; Quadrant III is the lower-left portion of the grid; and Quadrant IV is the lower-right portion. The four quadrants of the grid start in the upper-right portion and move counterclockwise. Several sample points are plotted on the following grid to illustrate these ideas.

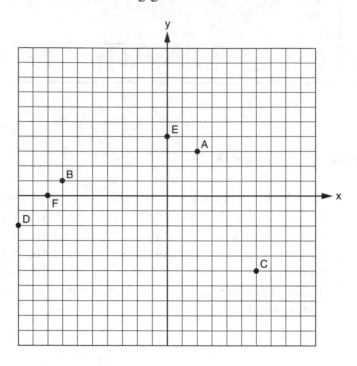

- *A* has coordinates $(2, 3)$.
- *B* has coordinates $(^-7, 1)$.
- *C* has coordinates $(6, -5)$.
- *D* has coordinates $(-10, -2)$.
- *E* has coordinates $(0, 4)$.
- *F* has coordinates $(-8, 0)$.

Notice that when its *x*-coordinate is 0, a point lies on the *y*-axis, and when its *y*-coordinate is 0, a point lies on the *x*-axis.

Applications of Coordinate Geometry

Now let's see how segments can be located on a grid. You can name the coordinates of the endpoints of each segment. For example, segment s_1 in the following figure has endpoints $(1, ^-4)$ and $(1, 2)$; segment s_2 has endpoints $(^-7, ^-4)$ and $(1, ^-4)$; and segment s_3 has endpoints $(^-7, ^-4)$ and $(1, 2)$.

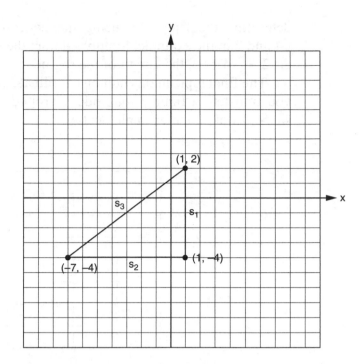

These three segments form a triangle because all three pairs of segments have a common endpoint. The vertices (plural of vertex) of this triangle are ($^-$7, $^-$4), (1, 2), and (1, $^-$4).

When a segment is parallel to one of the axes, it's easy to measure its length. Just count the number of spaces. For example, segment s_1 is 6 units long and segment s_2 is 8 units long. You can use the Pythagorean Theorem to find the length of s_3 because the triangle is a right triangle:

$$s_3^2 = s_1^2 + s_2^2$$

$$s_3^2 = 6^2 + 8^2$$

$$s_3^2 = 36 + 64$$

$$s_3^2 = 100$$

$$s_3 = \sqrt{100} = 10$$

Therefore, the perimeter of this triangle is $6 + 8 + 10 = 24$.
You can also find the area of this triangle:

$$A = \frac{1}{2}bh$$

$$A = \frac{1}{2}(8)(6)$$

$$A = 24\,units^2$$

The endpoints of a segment that is parallel to one of the axes have one common coordinate. The segment s_1 in the preceding example is parallel to the y-axis. Its endpoints are (1, $^-$4) and (1, 2), and the common coordinate is the x-coordinate 1. As stated earlier, you can determine the length of the segment by counting grid spaces between the endpoints. But you can also determine the length by using the coordinates that are not common, ⁻4 and 2 in the example. Simply subtract the smaller number from the larger: 2 − ⁻4 = 6, the length of the segment.

The final topic in this unit on coordinate geometry is **translation**. When you translate a figure, you slide it around the grid without changing its shape. Look at the example next.

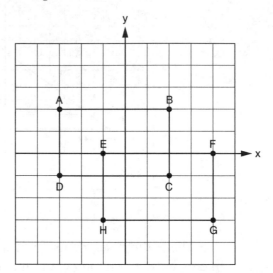

Any translation can be broken down into a horizontal part and a vertical part. In this example, you can see from the vertices that rectangle *ABCD* has moved 2 units to the right and 2 units down to make rectangle *EFGH*. Every point of rectangle *ABCD* has moved in this fashion. Rectangle *EFGH* is a translation of rectangle *ABCD* of plus 2 (right) and minus 2 (down).

Coordinate Geometry Practice

The diagram shows a rectangle on a coordinate grid. Use the diagram to answer questions 1−4.

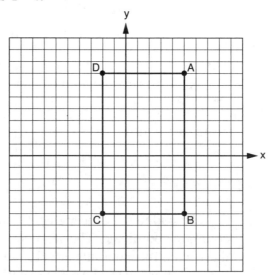

1. What are the coordinates of point *A*?

    a. (5, 7)   **b.** (⁻5, 7)   **c.** (7, 5)   **d.** (7, ⁻5)

2. What is the area of rectangle *ABCD*?

    a. 38 units^2 **b.** 104 units^2 **c.** 84 units^2 **d.** 52 units^2

3. Which of the following points lies outside the rectangle?

    a. (0, 0)   **b.** (3, 7)   **c.** (⁻3, 6)   **d.** (2, ⁻5)

4. What is the perimeter of rectangle *ABCD*?

    a. 38 units   **b.** 84 units   **c.** 104 units   **d.** 52 units

The diagram shows a triangle on a rectangular grid. Use the diagram to answer questions 5−8.

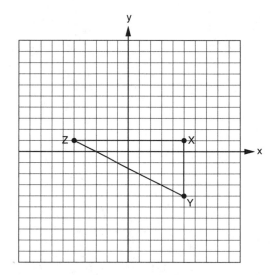

5. What type of triangle is in the diagram?

    a. isosceles   **b.** right   **c.** obtuse   **d.** equiangular

6. What is the area of triangle *XYZ*?

    a. 16 units^2 **b.** 32 units^2 **c.** 25 units^2 **d.** 18 units^2

7. What are the coordinates of point *Z*?

    a. (5, 1)   **b.** (⁻5, 1)   **c.** (⁻5, 0)   **d.** (5, 0)

8. What is the correct way to describe the values of the coordinates of most of the points $\overline{XY}$?

    a. *x* is positive and *y* is positive.

    b. *x* is positive and *y* is negative.

    c. *x* is negative and *y* is positive.

    d. *x* is negative and *y* is positive.

What Is Data Analysis?

Data analysis is the process of deriving meaning from numbers. There are two types of data. **Quantitative data** are numbers that reflect some characteristic of a group. Heights or weights, test scores, ages, and so on, are examples of quantitative data. **Categorical data** are labels that reflect categories. These labels can be names or numbers. For example, hair color, breed of dog, gender, or hurricane category (such as a Category 3 hurricane) are examples of categorical data.

This lesson begins with methods of summarizing data, using data to find probabilities, and counting cases in possibly overlapping categorical data sets. The lesson then looks at the presentation of data in charts, tables, and graphs and the analysis of data in these forms using methods described in previous lessons.

Summarizing Data

One of the first things you do with a data set is to summarize it. One way to do this for quantitative data is to represent the whole data set with a single number. A single number such as this is loosely called the "average" of a data set. Statisticians actually measure "average" in three different ways. These are called **measures of central tendency**.

The **mean** of a data set is what most people think of when they hear the word "average." Add up the numbers and divide by how many numbers there are. For example, suppose you have five golf scores for nine holes: 39, 40, 45, 43, and 45. The mean is $(39 + 40 + 45 + 43 + 45) \div 6 = 42.4$. You can only calculate the mean of quantitative data.

The **median** of a data set is the *middle number* when the numbers are in order from smallest to largest. The five golf scores in order are 39, 40, 43, 45, and 45. The median is 43. The median is less sensitive to the high and low values in the data set. If, for instance, one score of 45 were 55 instead, the median would still be 43, but the mean would increase to 44.4. The median also only applies to quantitative data.

You might have noticed that a list of numbers only has a middle number when the list is an odd number in length. Suppose there are six golf scores instead of five: 39, 40, 45, 43, 45, and 41. Listed in order: 39, 40, 41, 43, 45, and 45. When a list is an even number in length, there are two middle scores—in this case 41 and 43. The median is the mean of these two middle scores—in this case $(41 + 43) \div 2 = 42$.

The **mode** of a data set is the most frequently occurring number in the case of quantitative data. In the golf score case, the mode is 45 because that number appears in the list twice while all the other numbers are only in the list once. For categorical data, the mode is the most frequently occurring category. If a certain group of women consisted of 15 brunettes, 7 blondes, and 5 redheads, the mode would be "brunette."

Practice Summarizing Data

1. Last week there were 42, 35, 37, 41, 29, 26, and 38 customers in Pizzola's Restaurant. Find the median number of customers.

2. The local police department reported the mean number of 18.6 car thefts per month in 2005. What is the mean number of reported car thefts that year?

3. Chinn got scores of 95, 90, 89, and 85 on four math tests. What score does he need on the fifth test to have an average of 90?

4. Hank's Hardware reported daily receipts of $350.23, $803.27, $647.39, $893.48, and $1480. The accountant discovered an error in the last amount—it should have been $4180. Which is affected less—the mean or the median?

5. At a recent dog show, there were 8 German shepherds, 5 collies, 12 poodles, and 9 beagles. What was the modal category?

Probability

The concept of **probability** is most easily understood by example.

Example A. Of 135 teachers at a certain high school, 86 are registered as Democrat, 38 as Republican, and 11 as Independent. What is the probability that a randomly selected teacher is Republican?

Divide the number of registered Republican teachers by the total number of teachers: $\frac{38}{135} \approx 0.28$. You can also state a probability as a percent, in this case 28%.

Example B. A die is rolled. What is the probability that the side facing up is less than 3?

A die has six sides, numbered 1 through 6. Two of these, 1 and 2, are less than three. The desired probability is $\frac{2}{6} = \frac{1}{3} = 0.33 = 33\%$.

Example C. George has 5 pair of boxer shorts and 8 pair of briefs in his underwear drawer. If he reaches in without looking, what is the probability that he will pull out a pair of briefs?

George has 13 pair (8 + 5) of underwear altogether. Since 8 pair are briefs, the desired probability is $\frac{8}{13} \approx 0.62 = 62\%$.

Probability Practice

1. Grace has 35 yellow and 28 red roses randomly placed in her garden. She is blindfolded, led into her garden, and is asked to pick a rose (wearing garden gloves, of course!) What is the probability that she picks a yellow one?

2. What is the probability of getting a number less than 3 on the spinner?

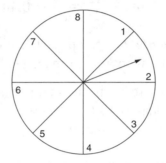

3. There were 13 men and 18 women in the class. A class member was chosen at random. What is the probability that it was a woman?

4. A bag of M&Ms contains 8 brown, 5 green, 4 red, and 2 yellow. An M&M is randomly picked. What is the probability that it is red?

5. Lucas has a free-throw shooting percentage of 88%. If he takes a free throw, what is the probability that Lucas will miss it?

Counting Cases of Categorical Data

A **Venn diagram** is a picture that helps you keep track of the number of cases there are in each of two possibly overlapping categories. An example of a Venn diagram is shown next.

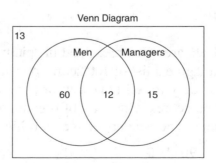

Venn Diagram

The circle on the left represents men who work for a certain company, and the circle on the right represents managers who work at that company. The overlap in the center of the diagram represents men who are also managers. There are 12 men who are managers, 60 men who are not managers, and 15 managers who aren't men. The space outside both circles represents people who work for the company who are neither men nor managers.

Example D. Use this Venn diagram to find the probability that a man selected at random is a manager.

There are 72 men in the company (60 + 12) and 12 men who are managers, so the desired probability is $\frac{12}{72} = \frac{1}{6} \approx 0.17 = 17\%$.

Example E. Find the probability that a randomly selected manager is a man. There are 27 managers (15 + 12) of which 12 are men, so this probability is $\frac{12}{27} = \frac{4}{9} \approx 0.44 = 44\%$.

Example F. Suppose the company has 100 employees. How many are female who are not managers?

There are 87 in the company who are male or manager (60 + 12 + 15). This leaves 13 (1 − 87) who are neither male nor manager (that is, female and not a manager).

Counting Problems Practice

1. An office of 40 people consists of 5 redheaded women and 22 women. How many men are in the office?

2. A grocery store has 65 cases of Super Cola and 47 cases of sugar-free cola of all brands. Thirteen cases of the Super Cola are sugar free. How many cases of Super Cola and sugar-free cola does the store have altogether?

3. A parking lot has 50 cars in it. Twelve of the cars are gray, and 30 of the cars are foreign. Six are gray foreign cars. How many American cars in the lot are not gray?

4. A menu contains 6 fried items and 7 beef items. Three of the items contain fried beef. How many items are fried but do not contain beef?

Data Presentation

Data are often presented in "picture" form to make it easier to see patterns. Imagine a list of 100 scores on a test taken by college freshmen. It wouldn't be easy to tell how well or poorly the group did just by looking at names and scores. One way of organizing the scores is to put them in a table by tens. The headers of such a **table** might look like:

90–100	80–89	70–79	60–69	Below 60

The individual scores would be placed in these columns, and the lengths of the columns would give some indication of whether scores were generally good or not so good.

A second way of presenting test scores such as these would be to construct bars whose heights were proportional to the number of scores in each column of the table. A **bar chart** (or histogram) for a set of hypothetical scores is shown next.

Hypothetical Bar Chart of Test Scores

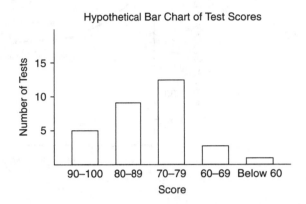

The scores could also be presented in a **pie chart**. This is a circular figure that is divided into regions shaped like pieces of pie whose areas are proportional to the number of scores represented by the region. A pie chart that depicts the same data as in the preceding bar chart is shown next.

Hypothetical Pie Chart of Test Scores

The test scores in the preceding examples are quantitative data. You could present categorical data in the same ways. Suppose you had a list of women's hair color (brunette, blonde, or redhead) instead of their test scores. You could construct a table with the headers:

<u>Brunette</u>   <u>Blonde</u>   <u>Readhead</u>

Then you could list the names of the people in the appropriate column. Again the lengths of the columns would give you some sense of the proportion of time each hair color is observed. Or these could be the categories in a bar chart or a pie chart.

A **line graph** is a good way to present numbers that measure some quantity over time. Fluctuations in the daily price of gasoline in some metropolitan area could be readily seen in a line graph. An example of this line graph is shown next.

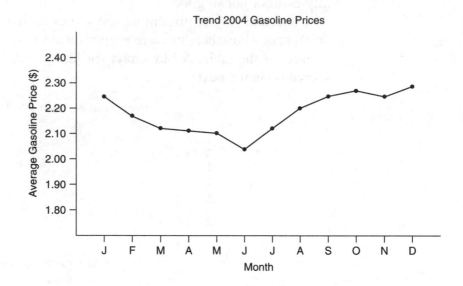

A **scatterplot** on a coordinate plane is a good way of visualizing the relationship between two variables. Suppose, for example, you had a list of 25 people with their number of years of education and their salaries. You could plot each person as a point on a coordinate plane, where the *x*-coordinate stands for years of education and the *y*-coordinate stands for annual salary. Such a scatterplot is shown next.

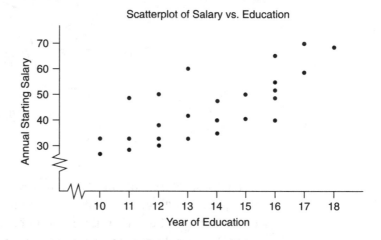

The fact that the dots seem to follow an upward trend from left to right indicates that higher salaries are associated with more years of education.

Another visual method of displaying data is in a **graph** on the coordinate plane. In the following example, time is measured on the *x*-axis, and distance is measured on the *y*-axis. Points on the graph show the distance traveled in amounts of time. The point *A,* for instance, represents a distance of 10 miles in a time of 20 minutes. The point *B* represents a distance of 10 miles in a time of 30 minutes, indicating a stop of 10 minutes.

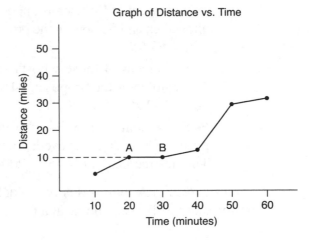

Graph of Distance vs. Time

Graphs can be used to picture a variety of relationships. If you were pouring water into a bottle shaped like the next one, you would expect the water to rise faster as time passed since the bottle narrows as you move up. This means the height of the water would increase more between the 3rd and 4th seconds than between the 1st and 2nd seconds. The graph would look something like this:

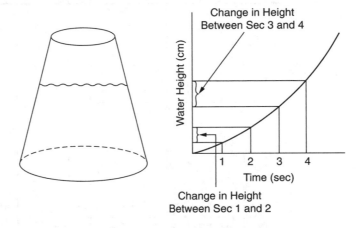

Tables and figures in the TABE A are often used as the basis for multiple questions spanning several topics. This is illustrated in the examples that follow.

Example G. Two hundred people were surveyed about a proposed gun control law. Among the questions asked were political party affiliation and whether or not the proposed law was favored. These results are summarized in the following table.

	Republican	Democrat	Total
Favor Proposal	64	45	109
Oppose Proposal	39	52	91
Total	103	97	200

1. What percent of Democrats oppose the proposal? There are 97 Democrats altogether, and 52 oppose the proposal. The percent opposed is 52 ÷ 97 × 100 ≈ 53.6%.

2. What percent of those who favor the proposal is Republican? Of the 109 who favor the proposal, 64 are Republican. The desired percent is 64 ÷ 109 × 100 ≈ 58.7%.

3. What percent of those surveyed are Democrats who favor the proposal? Of the 200 surveyed, 45 are Democrats who favor the proposal. The desired percent is 45 ÷ 200 × 100 = 22.5%.

Example H. A man walks two blocks to a store, spends 5 minutes in the store, and walks back home at a faster speed. Which graph shows this event?

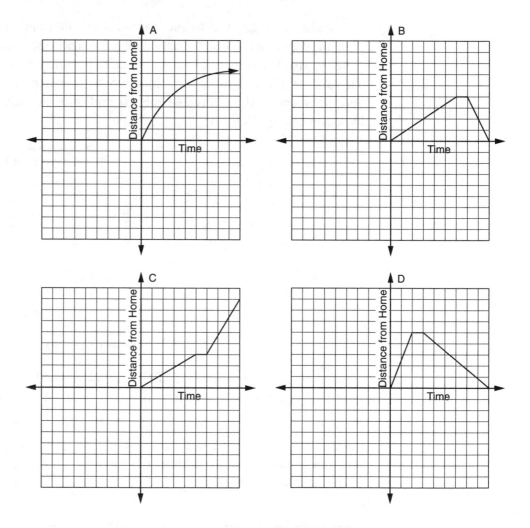

Graph A doesn't show the five minutes of stopping time. Graph C shows stopping time, but also shows the walk continuing away from home. Graph D shows the stopping time and the return home, but the walking speed is faster going to the store. The correct graph is B.

Example I. The following table shows the approximate monthly expenses for the Jones family. Use this table to answer questions 1–3.

Category	Cost
Housing	$670
Utilities	$240
Food	$325
Entertainment	$200
Medical	$125
Household	$140
Vehicle	$150
Miscellaneous	$140

1. Oil prices have caused the cost of utilities to go up by 15%. What is the new estimated expense for Utilities? We need to calculate 15% more than the current expense of $240. This will be $15 \times 240 \div 100 = 36$. Utilities will cost $36 more, or $276 per month.

2. Approximately what does it cost to run the Jones' vehicle for a year? It will cost $12 \times \$125 = \$1500$ a year for the Jones family to operate the vehicle.

3. Mr. and Ms. Jones have a combined monthly take-home income of $2500. After expenses, they put half in a savings account and half in a retirement account. How much goes into each account? Total expenses for the month are about $1950. This leaves $2500 - \$1950 = \$550$ to be split between the two accounts. Therefore, the Joneses put $225 into each account.

Example J.   The following pie chart shows the market share for each of three cable companies. Which company has more than half the market share?

Market Share for Three Cable Companies

Cross Cable takes more than half the pie chart. Therefore, they have more than half the market share.

Posttest

PART I: Mathematics Computation
Note: No calculator permitted

Date: _____   **Start Time:** _____

1. $6.11 - 3.24 =$

   A   3.97

   B   2.97

   C   2.87

   D   2.97

   E   None of these

2. $^-34 + 7 =$

   A $^-41$

   B   41

   C   27

   D $^-27$

   E   None of these

3. $0.04 + 0.0007 =$

   A   0.0407

   B   0.047

   C   0.0047

   D   0.47

   E   None of these

4. Solve for x: $x - 3 = 4$

   A $x = 1$

   B $x = 12$

   C $x = -1$

   D $x = 7$

   E   None of these

5. $8\frac{5}{7} - 5\frac{1}{7} =$

   A $3\frac{6}{7}$

   B $3\frac{4}{7}$

   C $3\frac{1}{7}$

   D $2\frac{4}{7}$

   E   None of these

6. 20% of $300 =
   A $6
   B $50
   C $60
   D $600

7. 37.28 − 0.752 =
   A 36.528
   B 36.56
   C 38
   D 3.032
   E None of these

8. $6\frac{4}{9} + 1\frac{1}{9} =$
   A $7\frac{5}{18}$
   B $6\frac{4}{81}$
   C $7\frac{5}{9}$
   D $7\frac{4}{9}$
   E None of these

9. $\sqrt{64} = ?$
   A 8
   B 16
   C 32
   D 48
   E None of these

10. $^-18 \div {}^-2 =$
    A 9
    B $^-9$
    C 8
    D $^-8$
    E None of these

11. $4^2 + 6^2$
    A 20
    B 52
    C 100
    D 576
    E None of these

12. $9 + {}^-4 + {}^-9$
    A $^-4$
    B $^-22$
    C 22
    D 4
    E None of these

13. $3^3 \times 2 =$
    A 18
    B 36
    C 54
    D 66
    E None of these

14. $12\overline{)6.00} =$
    A 0.5
    B 2
    C 5
    D 20
    E None of these

15. $0.4 \times 1000 =$
    A 4
    B 40
    C 400
    D 4000
    E None of these

16. $^-320 \div 8 =$

    A $^-4$

    B $^-40$

    C   4

    D   40

    E   None of these

17. 100% of _____ = 35

    A   0.35

    B   3.5

    C   35

    D   350

    E   None of these

18.
$$\begin{array}{r} 12\frac{2}{3} \\ -\ 5\frac{1}{9} \\ \hline \end{array}$$

    A $6\frac{1}{9}$

    B $6\frac{5}{9}$

    C $7\frac{1}{9}$

    D $7\frac{5}{9}$

    E   None of these

19. $1000 \times\ ^-1 =$

    A $^-1001$

    B $^-1000$

    C   999

    D   1001

    E   None of these

20. $20.7 \times 31 =$

    A   64.17

    B   83.7

    C   641.7

    D   6417

    E   None of these

21. $0 - 4 =$

    A $^-4$

    B $^-3$

    C   0

    D   4

    E   None of these

22. $20.6 - 5.06$

    A   15.54

    B   15.6

    C   15.66

    D   15.72

    E   None of these

23. $^-18 \times\ ^-5 =$

    A -90

    B $^-23$

    C   23

    D   90

    E   None of these

24.

$$5\frac{7}{12}$$
$$+\ 8\frac{1}{3}$$

A $13\frac{8}{15}$

B $13\frac{7}{12}$

C $13\frac{11}{12}$

D $14\frac{1}{12}$

E None of these

25. $\frac{14}{15} \div \frac{7}{15} =$

A $\frac{2}{15}$

B 2

C $\frac{15}{7}$

D $\frac{1}{2}$

E None of these

26. $45 \times \frac{1}{15} =$

A $\frac{1}{3}$

B 3

C $\frac{46}{15}$

D $\frac{15}{46}$

E None of these

27. $\frac{^-45}{^-5} =$

A $^-50$

B $^-9$

C 9

D 50

E None of these

28. $3 + (7 - 2)^2 =$

A 28

B 48

C 13

D 16

E None of these

29. $4 - {}^-7 =$

A $^-11$

B $^-3$

C 3

D 11

E None of these

30. $27.15 \div 0.3 =$

A 9.05

B 9.5

C 90.5

D 905

E None of these

31. 10.5% of 90 =

A 9.45

B 10

C 10.5

D 10.55

E None of these

32. $\sqrt{64} - \sqrt{16} =$

   A   4

   B $\sqrt{48}$

   C   24

   D $\sqrt{80}$

   E   None of these

33. $9 - 3 \times 2 + 8 =$

   A   7

   B   20

   C   24

   D   60

   E   None of these

34. $20 \div \dfrac{5}{4} =$

   A   1

   B   16

   C   25

   D   36

   E   None of these

35. What percent of 300 is 60?

   A   2%

   B   18%

   C   20%

   D   24%

   E   None of these

36. $(^-3 - {}^-8) \times {}^-2 =$

   A $^-22$

   B $^-10$

   C   10

   D   22

   E   None of these

37. $5\dfrac{2}{3} \times 3\dfrac{5}{8} =$

   A $15\dfrac{5}{12}$

   B $2\dfrac{5}{12}$

   C $20\dfrac{5}{12}$

   D $20\dfrac{13}{24}$

   E   None of these

38. 40% of _____ = 18

   A   7.2

   B   45

   C   52

   D   72

   E   None of these

39. Simplify $6(3x^2 + 2x) - 5x =$

   A $30x^3 - 5x$

   B $18x^2 - 7x$

   C $18x^2 + 7x$

   D $30x^3 + 5x$

   E   None of these

40. $2 + 5^2 \times 3 =$

   A   60

   B   77

   C   81

   D   147

   E   None of these

Part II. Applied Mathematics
Note. Calculator Permitted

Date: _____   Start Time: _____

1. Jim drives at an average of 48 miles per hour on a two-and-a-half-hour trip. How far does he travel?

   A   96 miles

   B   112 miles

   C   120 miles

   D   132 miles

2. What is 74.36 rounded to the nearest tenth?

   A   70.0

   B   74.0

   C   74.3

   D   74.4

3. What number is a factor of all the numbers shown next?

   12   18   27   42   63

   A   2

   B   3

   C   4

   D   5

The table shows the number of residents of East and West Springfield who agree or disagree with a proposal to build a new bridge connecting the two towns. Study the table. Then do problems 4–7.

Local Survey

	Residents of East Springfield	Residents of West Springfield
Agree	175	250
Disagree	100	500

4. If a resident of East Springfield who participated in the survey is selected at random, what is the probability that this resident disagrees with the proposal?

   A $\dfrac{1}{3}$

   B $\dfrac{4}{11}$

   C $\dfrac{7}{11}$

   D $\dfrac{5}{6}$

5. What percent of all those surveyed agree with the proposal?

   A   about 30%

   B   about 71%

   C   about 40%

   D   about 50%

6. Which graph shows how the West Springfield residents voted in the survey?

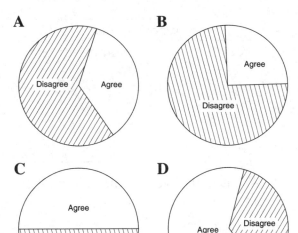

A

B

C

D

7. If the new bridge is built, it will take on average about 15 minutes to drive from one town center to the other. Now you have to drive 25 miles at an average speed of 50 miles per hour. How much driving time would be saved driving between the two town centers with the new bridge?

A 10 minutes

B 15 minutes

C 20 minutes

D 25 minutes

8. What is the supplement of a 70° angle?

A 20°

B 30°

C 90°

D 110°

9. Bill expects to get an 8% raise with his next paycheck. If his gross pay (before deductions) is $3550 per month, what will it be after his raise?

A $3834 per month

B $4118 per month

C $5176 per month

D $6030 per month

10. Rich noticed one month that his cable bill was $43.56 and his telephone bill was $55.24. Approximately how much does Rich pay for cable and telephone in a year?

A $800

B $900

C $1000

D $1200

11. A group of hikers observed that their altitude was 4635 feet at 10:30 A.M. and 3954 feet at 2:30 P.M. What was their change in altitude during the four hours?

A 681 feet

B ⁻681 feet

C 781 feet

D ⁻781 feet

12. Four members of a bowling team went for dinner to celebrate a big win. The cost was $73.68 including tax and tip. If they left a 20% tip, how much was the dinner including tax?

A $58.91

B $61.40

C $66.28

D $66.95

13. Once a month, Clyde plans to put an amount d into a savings account and twice that amount into a retirement account. If P represents the amount of his monthly paycheck, which expression shows the amount of money he will have left from his paycheck after contributing to his savings and retirement accounts?

A $P - d + 2d$

B $P - (^-d - 2d)$

C $P - (d + 2d)$

D $P - (d - 2d)$

14. If this pattern continues, which of the figures following will be next?

A

B

C

D

15. The table next shows the number of visits to a certain website over a 5-week period.

Website Visits	
Week	Number of Visits
1	3842
2	2987
3	3612
4	3015
5	2909

What is the weekly median number of visits?

A   3612

B   3015

C   3273

D   2958

16. A fleet consists of 200 vehicles, of which $\frac{2}{5}$ are full-size cars and the rest are trucks. To reduce costs, the company plans to replace half of the full-size cars with compact cars. How many compact cars will the company buy?

A   20

B   40

C   60

D   80

17. The table following shows the average scores of six math tests taken in two neighboring high schools.

Test Scores at North and South High Schools

School	Test 1	Test 2	Test 3	Test 4	Test 5
North High	68	72	55	75	56
South High	73	85	63	86	68

In how many tests did South average more than 8 points more than North?

A 1

B 2

C 3

D 4

18. The table following shows information about the five most severe hurricanes to hit the United States.

Five Deadliest U.S. Hurricanes

Location	Date	Category	Approx. Number of Deaths
Galveston, Texax	1900	4	8000
Lake Okechobee, Florida	1928	4	2500
Louisiana/Miss. Coast	2005	3	1800
Florida Keys	1919	4	600
New England	1938	3	600

According to the table, which two areas experienced the most recent hurricanes?

A Galveston, Lake Okeechobee

B New England, Louisiana/Miss. Coast

C Galveston, Florida Keys

D Florida Keys, Okeechobee

19. Which equation means the same as 4 less than 8 times a number equals 9?

A $4 - 8x = 9$

B $4 + 8x = 9$

C $8x - 4 = 9$

D $8 + 4x = 9$

20. A local deli charges $3.99 a pound for boiled ham and $6.98 a pound for roast beef. Michelle has $15.00. Which inequality represents the amount (A) Michelle can spend on roast beef if she buys two pounds of boiled ham?

A $A \leq \$15.00 - (\$3.99 \times 2)$

B $A \geq \$15.00 - (\$6.98 \times 2)$

C $A \leq \$15.00 + (\$3.99 \times 2)$

D $A \leq \$15.00 - (\$6.98 \times 2)$

21. Jack has 6 brown socks, 4 black socks, and 3 blue socks in a drawer. If he selects a sock from the drawer at random, what is the probability that the sock will be blue or brown?

A $\dfrac{1}{3}$

B $\dfrac{4}{9}$

C $\dfrac{5}{9}$

D $\dfrac{9}{13}$

22. Of the 160 nurses at Eastside Hospital, $\frac{7}{8}$ work full time. Of the full time employees, $\frac{1}{5}$ regularly work overtime. How many nurses at Eastside Hospital regularly work overtime?

A   28

B   32

C   35

D   40

23. What is the volume of the box shown next?

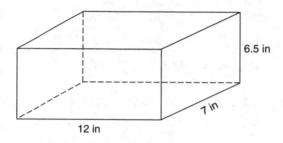

6.5 in

7 in

12 in

A   25.5 cubic inches

B   247 cubic inches

C   546 cubic inches

D   824 cubic inches

24. What number is missing from the number pattern?

1, 2, 5, 10, ——, 26, 37

A   15

B   17

C   19

D   21

25. Peter had a job to count the number of cars passing an intersection each hour. Starting at 9:00 A.M., he counted 86, 93, 96, 104, and 127 cars for the first five hours. He later realized that he transposed two digits and the last count should have been 172. Which of the following is not affected by this correction?

A   the range

B   the median

C   the mean

D   the mode

26. The cost of the meal at the 45-man golf league banquet was $853.92. If an 18% tip was added to the bill, which is the best estimate of the average cost per man?

A $17

B $22

C $27

D $32

The capacity of air conditioners to cool an area is measured in British thermal units (Btu). The table next shows the room areas that can be efficiently cooled by air conditioners of various capacities. Study the table. Then do problems 27–29.

Recommended Air Conditioner Capacities

Room Area (square feet)	Air Conditioner Capacity (Btu)
100–150	5,000
150–250	6,000
250–300	7,000
300–350	8,000
350–400	9,000
400–450	10,000
450–550	12,000
550–700	14,000

27. Which statement is supported by the data in the table?

    A   A 10,000 Btu air conditioner will work more efficiently in a larger room than a smaller room.

    B   Rooms smaller than 100 square feet shouldn't be air-conditioned.

    C   The size of a room should be considered when selecting the most efficient air conditioner.

    D   An 18,000 Btu air conditioner will cool any size room.

28. An air conditioner in a kitchen needs an additional 4000 Btu over the recommended capacity. What air conditioner capacity is required for a kitchen that has a length of 18 feet and a width of 12 feet?

    A   7000 Btu

    B   8000 Btu

    C   9000 Btu

    D   10,000 Btu

29. Kim bought an air conditioner that was on sale at 25% off. The model that she selected originally sold for $388.95. How much did Kim save at this sale?

    A $9.72

    B $25

    C $97.24

    D $291.71

The graph shows figures on a coordinate grid. Study the graph. Then do problems 30–32.

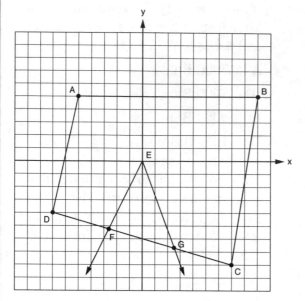

The graph shows the average ages of men and women at first marriage in Unionville for the years 1995–2002.

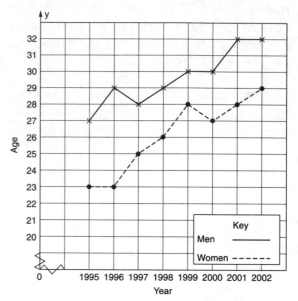

30. What is the length of $\overline{AB}$?

   A   4 units

   B   5 units

   C   9 units

   D   14 units

31. What is the correct way to describe the values of the coordinates of most of the points on $\overline{BC}$?

   A x is positive and y is positive.

   B x is positive and y is negative.

   C x is negative and y is positive.

   D x is negative and y is negative.

32. Which of these segments lies on a ray?

   A $\overline{AB}$

   B $\overline{BC}$

   C $\overline{EG}$

   D $\overline{AD}$

33. What was the average age at first marriage for women in 1998?

   A   26

   B   27

   C   28

   D   29

34. In how many years did the difference between men's and women's ages at first marriage decrease?

   A   1 year

   B   2 years

   C   3 years

   D   4 years

35. If the age of men at first marriage changes by the same amount from 2002 to 2003 as it did from 1997 to 1998, what will that age be in 2003?

   A 32 years

   B 33 years

   C 34 years

   D 35 years

The diagram shows a circle with center *C* and several labeled points. Study the diagram and work problems 36 and 37.

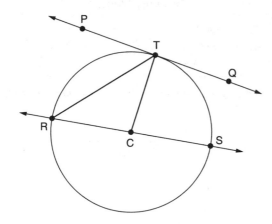

36. Which of these is a tangent to the circle?

   A $\overline{CT}$

   B $\overline{RS}$

   C $\overline{RT}$

   D $\overline{PQ}$

37. If $\overline{RS}$ has a length of 8 centimeters, what is the circumference *C* of the circle? ($C = 2\pi r$)

   A 2π centimeters

   B 8π centimeters

   C 16π centimeters

   D 24π centimeters

The diagram shows a triangle and a rectangle on a coordinate grid. Use the diagram to do problems 38–42.

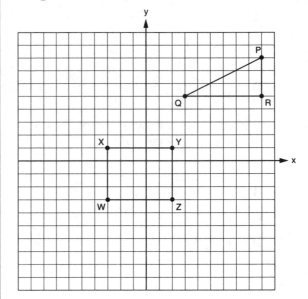

38. What is the perimeter of rectangle *XYZW*?

   A 9 units

   B 18 units

   C 20 units

   D 24 units

39. What are the coordinates of point *Q*?

   A ($^-$3, 5)

   B (3, $^-$5)

   C (3, 5)

   D ($^-$3, $^-$5)

40. What is the area of triangle *PQR*?

   A 9 square units

   B 18 square units

   C 19 square units

   D 20 square units

41. If rectangle *XYZW* is translated 4 units down, what is the new location of point *W*?

A   (3, ⁻7)

B   (⁻3, ⁻7)

C   (1, ⁻7)

D   (⁻7, ⁻7)

42. Which of the following points lies on the rectangle *XYZW*?

A   (2, 1)

B   (1, ⁻2)

C   (⁻2, ⁻2)

D   (⁻5, 3)

The back of a package of oatmeal contains facts about nutrition as well as directions for cooking the oatmeal. Study the information. Then do problems 43–46.

Nutrition Facts	
Serving size:	1/2 cup dry (40g)
Servings per container:	about 30

Amount Per Serving	
Calories	150
Calories from Fat	25

% Daily Value*	
Total Fat 3g	4%
Sodium 0 mg	0%
Total Carbohydrate 27 g	9%

* Percent Daily Values are based on a 2000 calorie diet.

Cooking Directions		
Servings	2	4
Water (or milk)	1 3/4	3 1/2
Oats (cups)	1	2
Salt (teaspoons)	1/4	1/2
Butter (tablespoons)	3/4	1 1/2

43. Dale plans to cook exactly 7 servings of oatmeal. According to the cooking directions, how many teaspoons of salt should she add to the uncooked oats?

A $\dfrac{7}{8}$

B $1\dfrac{1}{7}$

C $1\dfrac{3}{4}$

D $\dfrac{3}{4}$

44. A stick of butter contains 8 tablespoons of butter. What percent of a stick of butter is being used if 3 tablespoons of butter are used to cook the oatmeal?

A 25%

B 30%

C 37.5%

D 45%

45. Ann measures 7 cups of water to cook oatmeal for breakfast. According to the cooking directions, how much dry oatmeal should be added to the water?

A 2 cups

B $2\frac{1}{2}$ cups

C 3 cups

D 4 cups

46. Pam is an athlete and is on a strict daily diet of 3000 calories. What percent of her daily calorie requirement is met by the calories from two servings of oatmeal?

A 5%

B 10%

C 15%

D 20%

47. What value of x will make the inequality true?

$3x - 2 \geq 7$

A $x > 9$

B $x > 3$

C $x \geq 3$

D $x \geq 9$

48. What is the next number in this number sequence?

5, 1, −4, _____, −17, −25

A −9

B −10

C −11

D −12

49. Which equation is equivalent to the equation that follows?

$6x - 2y = 8$

A $y = 3x - 4$

B $y = {}^-3x + 4$

C $y = 3x - 8$

D $y = {}^-3x + 8$

50. The speed of light is approximately 11,160,000 miles per minute. What is the scientific notation for the distance light travels in an hour?

A 1.116×10^7 miles per hour

B 11.16×10^6 miles per hour

C 6.696×10^8 miles per hour

D 66.96×10^7 miles per hour

Posttest Answer Key, Lesson Key, and Problem Type
Part I. Mathematics Computation

Question	Answer	Lesson	Problem type
1	C	1	Subtracting decimals
2	D	3	Adding integers
3	A	1	Adding decimals
4	D	6	Solving equations
5	B	2	Subtracting mixed numbers
6	C	4	Finding the part in a percent problem
7	A	1	Subtracting decimals
8	C	2	Adding mixed numbers
9	A	5	Evaluating square roots
10	A	3	Dividing integers
11	B	5	Evaluating numerical expressions
12	A	3	Adding integers
13	C	5	Evaluating numerical expressions
14	A	1	Dividing decimals
15	C	1	Multiplying decimals
16	B	3	Dividing integers
17	C	4	Finding the whole in a percent problem
18	D	2	Subtracting mixed numbers
19	B	3	Multiplying integers
20	C	1	Multiplying decimals
21	A	3	Subtracting integers
22	A	1	Subtracting decimals
23	D	3	Multiplying integers
24	C	2	Adding mixed numbers
25	B	2	Dividing fractions
26	B	2	Multiplying fractions
27	C	3	Dividing integers
28	A	5	Evaluating numerical expressions
29	D	3	Subtracting integers
30	C	1	Dividing decimals
31	A	4	Finding the part in a percent problem
32	A	5	Evaluating square roots
33	E	5	Evaluating numerical expressions
34	B	2	Dividing fractions
35	C	4	Finding the % in a percent problem
36	B	3, 5	Evaluating numerical expressions
37	D	2	Multiplying mixed numbers
38	B	4	Finding the total in a percent problem
39	C	6	Simplifying expressions
40	B	5	Evaluating numerical expressions

Part II. Applied Mathematics

Question	Answer	Lesson	Problem type
1	C	7	Story problem involving travel
2	D	1	Rounding
3	B	1	Finding factors
4	B	12	Probability/Statistics
5	C	12	Probability/Statistics
6	A	12	Circle graph
7	B	7	Story problem on travel
8	D	9	Geometry definitions
9	A	7	Story problem on percent
10	D	7	Story problem on decimals
11	B	7	Story problem on integers
12	B	7	Story problem on percent
13	C	8	Words to symbols
14	A	8	Picture patterns
15	B	12	Summarizing data—median
16	B	7	Story problem on proportion
17	C	12	Data interpretation
18	B	12	Data interpretation
19	C	8	Words to symbols
20	A	8	Words to symbols
21	D	12	Probability/Statistics
22	A	7	Story problem on fractions
23	C	9	Volume of a prism
24	B	8	Number patterns
25	B	12	Summarizing data
26	B	7	Tipping
27	C	12	Data interpretation
28	D	9, 12	Data interpretation
29	C	7	Story problem on discount
30	D	11	Coordinate geometry
31	B	11	Coordinate geometry
32	C	11	Coordinate geometry
33	A	12	Interpreting a line graph
34	C	12	Interpreting a line graph
35	B	12	Interpreting a line graph
36	D	9	Geometry definitions
37	B	9	Area of a circle
38	B	9	Perimeter of a rectangle
39	C	11	Coordinate geometry
40	A	9	Area of a triangle

Question	Answer	Lesson	Problem type
41	B	11	Coordinate geometry
42	A	11	Coordinate geometry
43	A	12	Data interpretation
44	C	7	Story problem involving percent
45	D	7	Story problem involving proportions
46	B	7, 12	Data interpretation
47	C	6	Solving inequalities
48	B	8	Number patterns
49	A	6	Equivalent equations
50	C	1	Scientific notation

Posttest Answer Explanations
Part I Mathematics Computation

1. C   2.87   Line up the decimal points and subtract.

2. D   ⁻27   When adding numbers with different signs, ignore the signs and subtract the smaller number from the larger one. The answer has the sign of the larger number.

3. A   0.0407   Line up the decimal points, attach zeros at the end of the shorter number, and add.

4. D   7   Add 3 to both sides of the equation: $x - 3 + 3 = 4 + 3$. The result is $x = 7$.

5. B $3\frac{4}{7}$ First change the mixed numbers to improper fractions: $8\frac{5}{7} - 5\frac{1}{7} = \frac{61}{7} - \frac{36}{7}$. Since the fractions have the same denominator, subtract the numerators: $\frac{61}{7} - \frac{36}{7} = \frac{25}{7}$. As a mixed number, $\frac{25}{7} = 3\frac{4}{7}$.

6. C $60   You are looking for the part in a percent problem.
$$Part = \% \times Whole \div 100 = 20 \times 300 \div 100 = 60$$

7. A   36.528   Line up the decimal points, attach a zero to 37.28, and subtract.

8. C $7\frac{5}{9}$ First change the mixed numbers to improper fractions:
$6\frac{4}{9} + 1\frac{1}{9} = \frac{58}{9} + \frac{10}{9}$. Since the fractions have the same denominators, add the numerators: $\frac{58}{9} + \frac{10}{9} = \frac{68}{9}$. As a mixed number $\frac{68}{9} = 7\frac{5}{9}$.

9. A   8 $\sqrt{64} = 8$ because $8^2 = 8 \times 8 = 64$.

10. A   9   When dividing number with the same sign, the answer is positive.

11. B   52 $4^2 + 6^2 = (4 \times 4) + (6 \times 6) = 52$.

12. A   ⁻4   First add 9 and ⁻4 to get 5. (Ignore the signs, subtract the smaller number from the larger one, and give the answer the sign of the larger one.) Then add 5 and ⁻9 to get ⁻4. (Same rule.)

13. C   54 $3^3 \times 2 = (3 \times 3 \times 3) \times 2 = 54$.

14. A   0.5   Do the division, and place the decimal point above the one in the dividend.

15. C   400   Since 1000 has 3 zeros, move the decimal point 3 places to the right and fill in with zeros.

16. B   ⁻40   When dividing numbers with opposite signs, the answer is negative.

17. C   35   You are looking for the whole in a percent problem: 100% of the whole is the whole. So the whole is 35. Or use the formula:
$$Whole = Part \times \% \div 100 = 35 \times 100 \div 100 = 35.$$

18. D $7\frac{5}{9}$ First change the numbers to improper fractions:

$12\frac{2}{3} - 5\frac{1}{9} = \frac{38}{3} - \frac{46}{9}$. Since the denominators are different, you need a common denominator. The smallest number that both 3 and 9 divide into evenly is 9, so 9 is the least common denominator. The denominator of $\frac{46}{9}$ is already 9, so nothing has to be done to this number. To change the denominator of $\frac{38}{3}$ to 9, multiply both numerator and denominator by 3: $\frac{38}{3} = \frac{114}{9}$. Now subtract: $\frac{114}{9} - \frac{46}{9} = \frac{68}{9}$. Change $\frac{68}{9}$ by dividing, to get the mixed number $7\frac{5}{9}$.

19. B $^-1000$ When multiplying numbers with different signs, the answer is negative.

20. C 641.7 Multiply 207 by 31 and place the decimal point in one place from the right.

21. A $^-4$ $0 - 4 = 0 + {}^-4 = {}^-4$.

22. A 15.54 Line up the decimal points, attach a zero to 20.6, and subtract.

23. D 90 When multiplying numbers with the same sign, the answer is positive.

24. C $13\frac{11}{12}$ First change the mixed numbers to improper fractions:

$5\frac{7}{12} + 8\frac{1}{3} = \frac{67}{12} + \frac{25}{3}$. Since the denominators are different, you need a common denominator. The smallest number that both 12 and 3 divide evenly into is 12, so 12 is the least common denominator. The denominator of $\frac{67}{12}$ is already 12, so nothing has to be done to this number. To change the denominator of $\frac{25}{3}$ to 9, multiply both numerator and denominator by 4: $\frac{25}{3} = \frac{100}{12}$. Now add:

$\frac{67}{12} + \frac{100}{12} = \frac{167}{12}$. Change $\frac{167}{12}$ by dividing, to get the mixed number $13\frac{11}{12}$.

25. B 2 To divide, multiply by the reciprocal: $\frac{14}{15} \div \frac{7}{15} = \frac{{}^2\cancel{14}}{{}_1\cancel{15}} \times \frac{\cancel{15}^1}{\cancel{7}_1} = \frac{2}{1} = 2$.

26. B 3 The number 45 is equal to $\frac{45}{1}$, and to multiply fractions, multiply the numerators and multiply the denominators: $\frac{\cancel{45}^3}{1} \times \frac{1}{\cancel{15}_1} = \frac{3}{1} = 3$.

27. C 9 When dividing numbers with the same sign, the answer is positive.

28. A 28 Follow the order of operations. First subtract 2 from 7 inside the parentheses to get 5. Then raise 5 to the second power to get 25. Then add 3 to get 28: $3 + (7 - 2)^2 = 3 + 5^2 = 3 + 25 = 28$.

29. D 11 In this problem $^-7$ is subtracted from 4. To subtract, add the opposite. The opposite of $^-7$ is 7, and $7 + 4 = 11$.

30.	C	90.5	Multiply both dividend and divisor by 10 by moving each decimal point one place to the right :$27.15 \div 0.3 = 271.5 \div 3$. Then divide: $3\overline{)271.5} = 90.5$.

30. C 90.5 Multiply both dividend and divisor by 10 by moving each decimal point one place to the right :$27.15 \div 0.3 = 271.5 \div 3$. Then divide: $\dfrac{90.5}{3\overline{)271.5}}$.

31. A 9.45 You are looking for the part in a percent problem:
$Part = \% \times Whole \div 100 = 10.5 \times 90 \div 100 = 9.45.$

32. A 4 $\sqrt{64} = 8$ because $8^2 = 8 \times 8 = 64$, and $\sqrt{16} = 4$ because $4^2 = 4 \times 4 = 16$. $\sqrt{64} - \sqrt{16} = 8 - 4 = 4.$

33. E None of these Follow the order of operations by first multiplying $3 \times 2 = 6$. Then subtract 6 from 9 to get 3, and add 8 to get 11: $9 - 3 \times 2 + 8 = 9 - 6 + 8 = 3 + 8 = 11.$

34. B 16 The number 20 is $\dfrac{20}{1}$. Divide $\dfrac{20}{1}$ by $\dfrac{5}{4}$ means multiply $\dfrac{20}{1}$ by $\dfrac{4}{5}$: $\dfrac{\cancel{20}^4}{1} \times \dfrac{4}{\cancel{5}_1} = \dfrac{16}{1} = 16.$

35. C 20 You are looking for % in a percent problem:
$\% = Part \div Whole \times 100 = 60 \div 30 \times 100 = 20.$

36. B $^-10$ Follow the order of operations. First subtract $^-8$ from $^-3$ inside the parentheses by adding the opposite of $^-8$ to $^-3$: $^-3 - {}^-8 = {}^-3 + 8 = 5$. Then multiply this answer by $^-2$ to get $^-10$: $(^-3 - {}^-8) \times {}^-2 = (^-3 + 8) \times {}^-2 = 5 \times {}^-2 = {}^-10.$

37. D $20\frac{13}{24}$ First change to mixed numbers to improper fractions:
$5\frac{2}{3} \times 3\frac{5}{8} = \frac{17}{3} \times \frac{29}{8}$. Multiply the numerators and multiply the denominators to get $\frac{17}{3} \times \frac{29}{8} = \frac{493}{24}$. Then divide to get $20\frac{13}{24}$.

38. B 45 You are looking for the whole in a percent problem:
$Whole = Part \div \% \times 100 = 18 \div 40 \times 100 = 45.$

39. C $18x^2 + 7x$ First use the Distributive Property to multiply: $6(3x^2 + 2x) = 18x^2 + 12x$. Then subtract the like terms: $12x - 5x = 7x$, leaving $18x^2 + 7x.$

40. B 77 Follow the order of operations. First raise 5 to the second power: $5^2 = 5 \times 5 = 25$. Then multiply by 3: $25 \times 3 = 75$. Then add to 2 to get 77: $2 + 5^2 \times 3 = 2 + 25 \times 3 = 2 + 75 = 77.$

Part II Applied Mathematics

1. C 120 miles — Use the formula $d = rt$, where d stands for distance, r stands for speed, and t stands for time: $d = 48 \times 2.5 = 120$.

2. D 74.4 — The rounding digit in 74.36 is 3, and the digit to its right is 6. Since 6 is bigger than 5, increase the rounding digit by 1 to 4.

3. B 3 — The phrase "is a factor of" means the same thing as "divides evenly into." The number 3 is the only one that divides evenly into all of the numbers shown.

4. B $\frac{4}{11}$ — The number of East Springfield residents who disagree is 100, and the total number of East Springfield residents who were surveyed is $175 + 100 = 275$. The probability that an East Springfield resident disagrees is $\frac{100}{275} = \frac{4}{11}$.

5. C about 40% — The number of residents in both cities who agree with the proposal is $175 + 250 = 425$. The total number of residents surveyed is $175 + 250 + 100 + 500 = 1025$. The percent of those who agree is $\% = Part \div Whole \times 100 = 425 \div 1025 \times 100 \approx 40$.

6. A — Two-thirds of the circle in A is shaded to indicate "Disagree."

7. B 15 minutes — Use the formula $d = rt$: $25 = 50t$. Solve this equation for t by dividing both sides by 50: $\frac{25}{50} = \frac{50t}{50}$, so $t = \frac{25}{50} = \frac{1}{2}$ hour, or 30 minutes. Since it will only take 15 minutes with the new bridge, you would save 15 minutes.

8. D 110° — Two angles are supplements if their degree measures add up to 180. If one angle measures 70°, the other is $180° - 70° = 110°$.

9. A $3834 per month — The amount of the raise is the part in a percent problem. $Part = \% \times Whole \div 100 = 8 \times 3550 \div 100 = 284$. Add this to $3550 to get $3834.

10. D $1200 — The cable bill is $43.56, and the phone bill is $55.24. Together, this is $98.80, and $12 \times \$98.80 = \$1185.60$. The closest answer choice is D $1200.

11. B ⁻681 feet — Calculate the ending altitude minus the starting altitude: $3954 - 4635 = ⁻681$. The change is negative because they are coming down.

12. B $61.40   The tip is the part, and the cost of the meal including tax is the whole in a percent problem: *Part* = % × *Whole* ÷ 100, so *Tip* = 20 × *Cost* ÷ 100 = 0.2 × *Cost*. The total cost of the meal, including tax plus the tip, is $73.68: 1 × *Cost* + 0.2 × *Cost* = 73.68. This means that 1.2 × *Cost* = 73.68. Divide both sides of this equation by 1.2 to get $\frac{1.2 \times Cost}{1.2} = \frac{73.68}{1.2} = 61.40$.

13. C $P - (d + 2d)$ Clyde puts d into his savings account and $2d$ (twice d) into his retirement account. In all, he deducts $d + 2d$ from his paycheck. The amount left is $P - (d + 2d)$.

14. A   The shaded portion of the square moves around clockwise, so its next location is the upper-right corner.

15. B 3015   The median is the middle number when the numbers are arranged in order.

16. B 40   You need to calculate half of $\frac{2}{5}$ and multiply that number by 200:

$$\frac{1}{\cancel{2}} \times \frac{\cancel{2}^{1}}{\cancel{5}} \times \frac{\cancel{200}^{40}}{1} = \frac{40}{1} = 40.$$

17. C 3   South averaged more than 8 points higher than North in Tests 2, 4, and 5.

18. B New England, Louisiana/Miss. Coast   The dates 1938 and 2005 are the most recent.

19. C $8x - 4 = 9$ Eight times a number is $8x$, and 4 less than $8x$ is $8x - 4$. This last expression equals 9.

20. A $A \le \$15.00 - (\$3.99 \times 2)$ Michelle will spend $3.99 × 2 on 2 pounds of boiled ham. She started out with $15.00, so $15.00 − ($3.99 × 2) is the most she will have to spend on roast beef. Therefore, $A \le 15.00 - (\$3.99 \times 2)$.

21. D $\frac{9}{13}$ There are 6 + 4 + 3 = 13 socks in the drawer altogether, and 6 + 3 are blue or brown. The probability of picking a blue or brown sock is $\frac{9}{13}$.

22. A 28 $\frac{7}{8}$ of 160 is $\frac{7}{\cancel{8}} \times \frac{\cancel{160}^{20}}{1} = \frac{140}{1} = 140$ nurses work full time. $\frac{1}{5}$ of 140 is $\frac{1}{\cancel{5}} \times \frac{\cancel{140}^{28}}{1} = \frac{28}{1} = 28$ nurses work overtime.

23. C 546 cubic inches   Multiply the three dimensions together to find the volume: 12 × 7 × 6.5 = 546.

| 24. | B | 17 | Add 1 to the first number to get the second, 3 to the second number to get the third, 5 to the third number to get the fourth. Each step, the number added is 2 more than what is added the previous step. Therefore, add 7 to 10 to get 17. |

24. B 17 — Add 1 to the first number to get the second, 3 to the second number to get the third, 5 to the third number to get the fourth. Each step, the number added is 2 more than what is added the previous step. Therefore, add 7 to 10 to get 17.

25. B the median — Since there are 5 numbers, the median is the middle number when they are in order. The median is 96 whether the largest number is 127 or 172.

26. B $22 — The idea here is to use rounded numbers and computational shortcuts. If you round the total cost to $900 and divide by 45, you get $20 per man, without tip. (45 × 2 = 90, so 45 × 20 = 900.) So the cost per man, without tip is a little less than $20. Round the 18% tip up to 20%. The decimal value of 20% is 0.2, so the tip is a little less than 0.2 × 20 = 4. The per man cost of the meal and the tip is a little less than $20 plus a little less than $4. The closest answer choice is $22. (The exact answer is $22.39.)

27. C — The size of a room should be considered when selecting the most efficient air conditioner.
The table recommends air conditioners of specific capacities for different size rooms. This answer choice is self-explanatory.

28. D 10,000 Btu — An 18-foot by 12-foot kitchen has an area of 216 square feet. You need 4000 Btu more than the recommended capacity of 6000 for a room this size (6000 + 4000).

29. C $97.24 — You are looking for the part in a % problem:
$$Part = \% \times Whole \div 100 = 0.25 \times 388.95 = 97.24.$$

30. D 14 units — Starting at A, count the number of spaces until you get to B.

31. B x is positive and y is negative — Most of the points on $\overline{BC}$ are right of the y-axis (x is positive) and below the x-axis (y is negative).

32. C $\overline{EG}$ — A ray starts at a point and goes on forever in one direction. $\overline{EG}$ and $\overline{EF}$ are on rays, but only $\overline{EG}$ is an answer choice.

33. A 26 — The point on the dashed line above 1998 is at 26 on the vertical axis.

34. C 3 — The difference between men's and women's age at first marriage decreased when the graphs got closer together. This happened in 1996–1997, 1998–1999, and 2001–2002.

35. B 33 — The age at first marriage of men increased by one year in 1997–1998. If it increases by one year in 2002–2003, it will be 33 years in 2003.

36. D $\overline{PQ}$ — A tangent is a line that touches a circle in exactly one place.

37. B 8π centimeters — $\overline{RS}$ is a diameter, so the radius of the circle is half of 8, or 4. Substitute this into the equation for circumference: $C = 2\pi r = 2\pi(4) = 8\pi$.

38. B 18 units — The perimeter of a rectangle is twice the length plus twice the width: $P = 2l + 2w = 2(4) = 2(5) = 8 + 10 = 18$.

39.   C   (3, 5)   The point Q is 3 squares right of the *y*-axis (*x* is +3) and 5 squares above the *x*-axis (*y* is +5).

40.   A   9 square units   The formula for the area of a triangle is $A = \frac{1}{2}bh$, where *b* and *h* are the base and altitude of the triangle. Counting squares, $b = 6$ and $h = 3$, so $A = \frac{1}{2}\left(\frac{6}{1}\right)\left(\frac{3}{1}\right) = \frac{18}{2} = 9$.

41.   B   (⁻3, ⁻7)   If the rectangle is translated down 4 units, every point, including W, moves down 4 units. The coordinates of W are $(-3, -3)$. To move it down 4, subtract 4 from the *y*-coordinate, -3: $^-3 - 4 = {}^-3 + {}^-4 = {}^-7$.

42.   A   (2, 1)   The coordinates of the point Y are (2, 1), and Y is on the rectangle.

43.   A $\frac{7}{8}$ The directions call for $\frac{1}{4}$ teaspoon of salt for 2 servings. Divide by 2 to get the amount of salt for 1 serving: $\frac{1}{4} \div 2 = \frac{1}{4} \div \frac{2}{1} = \frac{1}{4} \times \frac{1}{2} = \frac{1}{8}$. The amount of salt needed for 7 servings is $\frac{7}{1} \times \frac{1}{8} = \frac{7}{8}$.

44.   C   37.5%   You are looking for the % in a percent problem: % = *Part* ÷ *Whole* × 100 = 3 ÷ 8 × 100 = 37.5.

45.   D   4   Since you would use $3\frac{1}{2}$ cups of water for 4 servings, and 7 is twice as much as $3\frac{1}{2}$, 7 cups of water make 8 servings. Since 2 cups of oats make 4 servings, you would need 4 cups of oats to make 8 servings.

46.   B   10%   According to the information chart, each serving has 150 calories. Two servings have 300 calories. You are looking for the % in a percent problem: % = *Part* ÷ *Whole* × 100 = 300 ÷ 3000 × 100 = 10.

47.   C $x \geq 3$ To solve this inequality for *x*, first add 2 to both sides of the inequality: $3x - 2 + 2 \geq 7 + 2$, so $3x \geq 9$. Then divide both sides by 3: $\frac{3x}{3} \geq \frac{9}{3}$. So $x \geq 3$.

48.   B   ⁻10 $5 - \underline{4} = 1$; $1 - \underline{5} = -4$. This suggests that you get the fourth number by subtracting one more than 5: $^-4 - \underline{6} = {}^-4 + {}^-6 = {}^-10$. To check, subtract 7 from $^-10$, and you do get $^-17$, the next number in the list.

49.   A $y = 3x - 4$ You have to solve for $6x - 2y = 8$ for *y*.
Add 2*y* to both sides of the equation: $6x - 2y + 2y = 2y + 8$
$6x = 2y + 8$.
Subtract 8 from both sides of the equation: $6x - 8 = 2y + 8 - 8$
$6x - 8 = 2y$.
Divide both sides of the equation by 2: $\frac{6x}{2} - \frac{8}{2} = \frac{2y}{2}$
$3x - 4 = y$ or $y = 3x - 4$.

50.   C 6.696×10^8 miles per hour   To change 11,160,000 to scientific notation, move the decimal point from the end of the number to the place that makes this number between 1 and 10. You had to move the decimal point 7 places to do this. So the scientific notation for 11,160,000 is 1.116×10^7. But this is miles per minute. The problem asks for miles per hour. So you have to multiply this answer by 60, or 6×10. Multiplying by 6 changes 1.116 to 6.696. Multiplying by 10 changes 10^7 to 10^8. The final result is 6.696×10^8.

Solutions and Answers

Lesson 1. Decimals

Writing Decimals Practice

1. $37 = 3 \times 10^1 + 7$
2. $75{,}021 = 7 \times 10^4 + 5 \times 10^3 + 2 \times 10^1 + 1$
3. $0.896 = 8 \times 10^{-1} + 9 \times 10^{-2} + 6 \times 10^{-3}$
4. $1.362 = 1 + 3 \times 10^{-1} + 6 \times 10^{-2} + 2 \times 10^{-3}$
5. $456.301 = 4 \times 10^2 + 5 \times 10^1 + 6 + 3 \times 10^{-1} + 1 \times 10^{-3}$
6. $7000 = 7 \times 10^3$
7. $4 \times 10^2 + 8 \times 10^1 + 3 = 483$
8. $2 \times 10^4 + 6 \times 10^2 + 5 \times 10^{-1} + 8 \times 10^{-2} = 20{,}600.58$
9. $4 \times 10^6 + 7 \times 10^4 + 3 + 4 \times 10^{-1} = 4{,}070{,}003.4$
10. $8 + 1 \times 10^{-1} = 8.1$

Scientific Notation Practice

1. $3{,}100{,}000 = 3.1 \times 10^6$
2. $0.792 = 7.92 \times 10^{-1}$
3. $150 = 1.5 \times 10^2$
4. $0.0000000000936 = 9.36 \times 10^{-11}$
5. $3.23 \times 10^{-6} = 0.00000323$
6. $8.5 \times 10^2 = 850$
7. $7{:}3765 \times 10^{-3} = 0.0073765$
8. $2.7945 \times 10^{10} = 27{,}945{,}000{,}000$

Decimal Arithmetic

1. $7.1 + 3.25 = 10.35$
2. $12.478 - 9.53 = 2.948$
3. $112.43 + 39.1 = 151.53$
4. $\$66.10 - \$13.47 = \$52.63$
5. $125.52 + 0.97 = 126.49$
6. $80.03 - 42.95 = 37.08$
7. $\$20.00 - \$8.46 = \$11.54$
8. $19.00 - 5.7 = 13.3$
9. $3.4 \times 3 = 10.2$
10. $\$12.60 \div 3 = \$4.20$
11. $2.5 \times 3.2 = 8$
12. $5.2 \div 0.2 = 26$
13. $12 \times 1.25 = 15$
14. $0.63 \div .21 = 3$

15. $7.5 \times 3 = 22.5$　　　**16.** $20 \div 0.5 = 40$
17. $0.15 \times \$30 = \$4.50$　　**18.** $2.04 \div 0.04 = 51$
19. $1.9 \times 0.2 = 0.38$　　**20.** $1.8 \div 0.09 = 20$

Rounding Practice

1. 58.4 to the nearest unit: 58
2. 0.568 to the nearest hundredth: 0.57
3. 2354 to the nearest ten: 2350
4. 345 to the nearest hundred: 300
5. 0.7205 to the nearest thousandth: 0.721
6. 0.1643 to the nearest tenth: 0.16
7. 12.58 to the nearest ten: 10
8. 0.111 to the nearest tenth: 0.1
9. 1765 to the nearest thousand: 2000
10. 17.855 to the nearest hundredth: 17.86

Lesson 2. Fractions

Practice Changing Between Improper Fractions,
Whole Numbers, and Mixed Numbers

1. $\frac{4}{3} = 1\frac{1}{3}$　　**2.** $\frac{7}{4} = 1\frac{3}{4}$　　**3.** $\frac{6}{5} = 1\frac{1}{5}$　　**4.** $\frac{8}{3} = 2\frac{2}{3}$

5. $\frac{9}{3} = 3$　　**6.** $\frac{5}{1} = 5$　　**7.** $\frac{12}{7} = 1\frac{5}{7}$　　**8.** $\frac{4}{2} = 2$

9. $\frac{15}{8} = 1\frac{7}{8}$　　**10.** $\frac{13}{10} = 1\frac{3}{10}$　　**11.** $\frac{11}{4} = 2\frac{3}{4}$　　**12.** $\frac{12}{3} = 4$

13. $1\frac{2}{3} = \frac{5}{3}$　　**14.** $2\frac{1}{2} = \frac{5}{2}$　　**15.** $4\frac{2}{5} = \frac{22}{5}$　　**16.** $1\frac{11}{12} = \frac{23}{12}$

17. $3\frac{1}{3} = \frac{10}{3}$　　**18.** $6\frac{1}{8} = \frac{49}{8}$　　**19.** $8\frac{3}{8} = \frac{67}{8}$　　**20.** $5\frac{7}{9} = \frac{52}{9}$

21. $9\frac{3}{5} = \frac{48}{5}$　　**22.** $8\frac{7}{10} = \frac{87}{10}$　　**23.** $3\frac{5}{9} = \frac{32}{9}$　　**24.** $7\frac{1}{4} = \frac{29}{4}$

Reducing Fractions Practice

1. $\frac{2}{6} = \frac{1}{3}$　　**2.** $\frac{5}{10} = \frac{1}{2}$　　**3.** $\frac{3}{12} = \frac{1}{4}$　　**4.** $\frac{2}{20} = \frac{1}{10}$

5. $\frac{10}{15} = \frac{2}{3}$　　**6.** $\frac{18}{24} = \frac{3}{4}$　　**7.** $\frac{15}{10} = \frac{3}{2}$　　**8.** $\frac{8}{12} = \frac{2}{3}$

9. $\frac{12}{4} = 3$　　**10.** $\frac{6}{16} = \frac{3}{8}$　　**11.** $\frac{9}{6} = \frac{3}{2}$　　**12.** $\frac{12}{20} = \frac{3}{5}$

Multiply Fractions Practice

1. $\dfrac{2}{5} \times \dfrac{3}{7} = \dfrac{6}{35}$

2. $\dfrac{3}{8} \times \dfrac{1}{4} = \dfrac{3}{32}$

3. $\dfrac{\cancel{3}^{1}}{{}_{1}\cancel{7}} \times \dfrac{\cancel{21}^{3}}{{}_{2}\cancel{4}} = \dfrac{3}{2} = 1\dfrac{1}{2}$

4. $\dfrac{1}{{}_{1}\cancel{3}} \times \dfrac{\cancel{6}^{2}}{7} = \dfrac{2}{7}$

5. $5 \times \dfrac{3}{4} = \dfrac{5}{1} \times \dfrac{3}{4} = \dfrac{15}{4} = 3\dfrac{3}{4}$

6. $\dfrac{5}{8} \times 2\dfrac{1}{3} = \dfrac{5}{8} \times \dfrac{7}{3} = \dfrac{35}{24} = 1\dfrac{11}{24}$

7. $\dfrac{\cancel{12}^{6}}{5} \times \dfrac{1}{\cancel{2}^{1}} = \dfrac{6}{5} = 1\dfrac{1}{5}$

8. $4 \times \dfrac{17}{12} = \dfrac{\cancel{4}^{1}}{1} \times \dfrac{17}{{}_{3}\cancel{12}} = \dfrac{17}{3} = 5\dfrac{2}{3}$

9. $3 \times 2\dfrac{1}{5} = \dfrac{3}{1} \times \dfrac{11}{5} = \dfrac{33}{5} = 6\dfrac{3}{5}$

10. $1\dfrac{3}{4} \times 2\dfrac{1}{2} = \dfrac{7}{4} \times \dfrac{5}{2} = \dfrac{35}{8} = 4\dfrac{3}{8}$

11. $5\dfrac{2}{3} \times \dfrac{6}{17} = \dfrac{\cancel{17}^{1}}{3} \times \dfrac{6}{{}_{1}\cancel{17}} = \dfrac{6}{3} = 2$

12. $\dfrac{\cancel{7}^{1}}{{}_{1}\cancel{11}} \times \dfrac{\cancel{11}^{1}}{{}_{1}\cancel{7}} = \dfrac{1}{1} = 1$

Dividing Fractions Practice

1. $\dfrac{2}{5} \div \dfrac{1}{3} = \dfrac{2}{5} \times \dfrac{3}{1} = \dfrac{6}{5} = 1\dfrac{1}{5}$

2. $\dfrac{5}{8} \div \dfrac{2}{5} = \dfrac{5}{8} \times \dfrac{5}{2} = \dfrac{25}{16} = 1\dfrac{9}{16}$

3. $\dfrac{12}{7} \div \dfrac{1}{2} = \dfrac{12}{7} \times \dfrac{2}{1} = \dfrac{24}{7} = 3\dfrac{3}{7}$

4. $\dfrac{4}{7} \div 2 = \dfrac{4}{7} \div \dfrac{2}{1} = \dfrac{\cancel{4}^{2}}{7} \times \dfrac{1}{{}_{1}\cancel{2}} = \dfrac{2}{7}$

5. $5 \div \dfrac{5}{9} = \dfrac{5}{1} \div \dfrac{5}{9} = \dfrac{\cancel{5}^{1}}{1} \times \dfrac{9}{{}_{1}\cancel{5}} = \dfrac{9}{1} = 9$

6. $1\dfrac{1}{2} \div \dfrac{3}{4} = \dfrac{3}{2} \div \dfrac{3}{4} = \dfrac{\cancel{3}^{1}}{{}_{1}\cancel{2}} \times \dfrac{\cancel{4}^{2}}{\cancel{3}_{1}} = \dfrac{2}{1} = 2$

7. $12 \div \dfrac{2}{3} = \dfrac{12}{1} \div \dfrac{2}{3} = \dfrac{\cancel{12}^{6}}{1} \times \dfrac{3}{{}_{1}\cancel{2}} = \dfrac{18}{1} = 18$

8. $2\frac{1}{5} \div 1\frac{2}{3} = \frac{11}{5} \div \frac{5}{3} = \frac{11}{5} \times \frac{3}{5} = \frac{33}{25} = 1\frac{8}{25}$

9. $6 \div 1\frac{1}{2} = \frac{6}{1} \div \frac{3}{2} = \frac{\cancel{6}^2}{1} \times \frac{2}{\cancel{3}_1} = \frac{4}{1} = 4$

10. $1 \div 3 = \frac{1}{3}$

11. $1 \div \frac{1}{3} = \frac{1}{1} \div \frac{1}{3} = \frac{1}{1} \times \frac{3}{1} = \frac{3}{1} = 3$

12. $\frac{1}{3} \div \frac{2}{3} = \frac{1}{\cancel{3}_1} \times \frac{\cancel{3}^1}{2} = \frac{1}{2}$

Practice Adding and Subtracting Fractions

1. $\frac{1}{5} + \frac{2}{5} = \frac{3}{5}$

2. $\frac{7}{9} - \frac{4}{9} = \frac{3}{9} = \frac{1}{3}$

3. $\frac{1}{2} + \frac{1}{3} = \frac{1 \times 3}{2 \times 3} + \frac{1 \times 2}{3 \times 2} = \frac{3}{6} + \frac{2}{6} = \frac{5}{6}$

4. $\frac{7}{8} - \frac{1}{4} = \frac{7}{8} - \frac{1 \times 2}{4 \times 2} = \frac{7}{8} - \frac{2}{8} = \frac{5}{8}$

5. $\frac{2}{3} + \frac{1}{5} = \frac{2 \times 5}{3 \times 5} + \frac{1 \times 3}{5 \times 3} = \frac{10}{15} + \frac{3}{15} = \frac{13}{15}$

6. $\frac{3}{4} - \frac{3}{10} = \frac{3 \times 5}{4 \times 5} - \frac{3 \times 2}{10 \times 2} = \frac{15}{20} - \frac{6}{20} = \frac{9}{20}$

7. $3 + \frac{7}{5} = 3 + 1\frac{2}{5} = 4\frac{2}{5}$

8. $4\frac{2}{3} - 2\frac{1}{2} = \frac{14}{3} - \frac{5}{2} = \frac{14 \times 2}{3 \times 2} - \frac{5 \times 3}{2 \times 3} = \frac{28}{6} - \frac{15}{6} = \frac{13}{6} = 2\frac{1}{6}$

9. $8\frac{3}{8} + 2\frac{5}{12} = 8 + 2 + \frac{3}{8} + \frac{5}{12} = 10 + \frac{3 \times 3}{8 \times 3} + \frac{5 \times 2}{12 \times 2}$

$\quad = 10 + \frac{9}{24} + \frac{10}{24} = 10\frac{19}{24}$

10. $2\frac{1}{3} - \frac{3}{5} = \frac{7}{3} - \frac{3}{5} = \frac{7 \times 5}{3 \times 5} - \frac{3 \times 3}{5 \times 3} = \frac{35}{15} - \frac{9}{15} = \frac{26}{15} = 1\frac{11}{15}$

11. $4\frac{2}{3} + 2\frac{1}{3} = 4 + 2 + \frac{1}{3} + \frac{2}{3} = 6 + \frac{3}{3} = 6 + 1 = 7$

12. $1\frac{1}{2} - \frac{3}{5} = \frac{3}{2} - \frac{3}{5} = \frac{3 \times 5}{2 \times 5} - \frac{3 \times 2}{5 \times 2} = \frac{15}{10} - \frac{6}{10} = \frac{9}{10}$

Practice Changing Between Fractions and Decimals

1. $\frac{1}{4} = 0.25$ **2.** $\frac{2}{3} = 0.67$ **3.** $\frac{7}{8} = 0.88$

4. $\frac{4}{5} = 0.8$ **5.** $\frac{9}{12} = \frac{3}{4} = 0.75$ **6.** $\frac{6}{7} = 0.86$

7. $0.6 = \frac{6}{10} = \frac{3}{5}$ **8.** $0.28 = \frac{28}{100} = \frac{7}{25}$ **9.** $0.65 = \frac{65}{100} = \frac{13}{20}$

10. $0.125 = \frac{125}{1000} = \frac{1}{8}$ **11.** $0.92 = \frac{92}{100} = \frac{23}{25}$ **12.** $1.5 = \frac{15}{10} = \frac{3}{2}$

Lesson 3. Integers

Practice Adding Integers

1. $^-4 + 8 = 4$ **2.** $5 + {}^-8 = {}^-3$ **3.** $^-6 + {}^-14 = {}^-20$
4. $7 + {}^-5 = 2$ **5.** $^-3 + 1 = {}^-2$ **6.** $^-7 + {}^-4 = {}^-11$
7. $1 + {}^-1 = 0$ **8.** $^-3 + 6 = 3$

Practice Subtracting Integers

1. $8 - {}^-3 = 8 + 3 = 11$ **2.** $^-4 - 13 = {}^-4 + {}^-13 = {}^-17$
3. $^-1 - {}^-8 = {}^-1 + 8 = 7$ **4.** $12 - {}^-1 = 12 + 1 = 13$
5. $3 - 15 = 3 + {}^-15 = {}^-12$ **6.** $^-7 - {}^-2 = {}^-7 + 2 + {}^-5$
7. $12 - 4 = 8$ **8.** $6 - {}^-6 = 6 + 6 = 12$

Practice Multiplying and Dividing Integers

1. $^-7 \times 4 = {}^-28$ **2.** $15 \div {}^-3 = {}^-5$ **3.** $9 \times {}^-22 = {}^-198$
4. $^-63 \div 7 = {}^-9$ **5.** $^-13 \times {}^-4 = 52$ **6.** $^-66 \div 11 = {}^-6$
7. $3 \times {}^-9 = {}^-27$ **8.** $^-54 \div {}^-6 = 9$ **9.** $72 \div {}^-12 = {}^-6$

Mixed Practice on Integers

1. $21 - {}^-8 = 21 + 8 = 29$ **2.** $^-35 \div 7 = {}^-5$
3. $^-19 + {}^-6 = {}^-25$ **4.** $^-20 \div {}^-5 = 4$
5. $^-32 - {}^-8 = {}^-32 + 8 = {}^-24$ **6.** $^-3 \times {}^-7 = 21$
7. $^-9 + {}^-13 = {}^-22$ **8.** $42 \times {}^-1 = {}^-42$
9. $^-7 + 12 = 5$

Lesson 4. Percent

Practice Solving Basic Percent Problems

Find	**Solution**
1. *Part*	*Part* = 12 × 50 ÷ 100 = 6
2. *%*	*%* = 9 ÷ 20 × 100 = 45
3. *Whole*	*Whole* = 10 ÷ 25 × 100 = 40
4. *%*	*%* = 7 ÷ 10 × 100 = 70
5. *Whole*	*Whole* = 9 ÷ 15 × 100 = 60
6. *Part*	*Part* = 8 × 300 ÷ 100 = 24
7. *%*	*%* = 9 ÷ 18 × 100 = 50
8. *Whole*	*Whole* = 12 ÷ 20 × 100 = 60
9. *Whole*	*Whole* = 7 ÷ 25 × 100 = 28
10. *Part*	*Part* = 90 × 150 ÷ 100 = 135

Practice Changing Between Percents
and Decimals and Fractions

1. $0.52 = 52\%$

2. $\frac{1}{8} = 0.125 = 12.5\%$

3. $0.007 = 0.7\%$

4. $\frac{1}{6} = 0.167 = 16.7\%$

5. $1.25 = 125\%$

6. $\frac{13}{25} = 0.52 = 52\%$

7. $0.035 = 3.5\%$

8. $\frac{2}{9} = 0.22 = 22.2\%$

9. $0.084 = 8.4\%$

10. $\frac{3}{2} = 1.5 = 150\%$

11. $0.0095 = 1\%$

12. $\frac{4}{10} = 0.4 = 40\%$

13. $26\% = 0.26$

14. $8\% = 0.08$

15. $79.2\% = 0.792$

16. $2.5\% = 0.025$

17. $130\% = 1.3$

18. $0.04\% = 0.0004$

19. $12\% = 0.12 = \frac{12}{100} = \frac{3}{25}$

20. $9\% = 0.09 = \frac{9}{100}$

21. $125\% = 1.25 = 1\frac{25}{100} = 1\frac{1}{4}$

22. $6.5\% = 0.065 = \frac{65}{1000} = \frac{13}{200}$

23. $0.1\% = 0.001 = \frac{1}{1000}$

24. $85.5\% = 0.855 = \frac{855}{1000} = \frac{171}{200}$

Lesson 5. Order of Operations

Practice Using Order of Operations

1. $1 + 6 \times 2 = 1 + 12 = 13$
2. $5^2 \times 3 - 1 = 25 \times 3 - 1 = 75 - 1 = 74$
3. $12 \div 2 \times 3 = 6 \times 3 = 18$
4. $(5 - 2) \times 4 = 3 \times 4 = 12$
5. $9 - (2 + 3) = 9 - 5 = 4$
6. $3(8 + 2^3) = 3(8 + 8) = 3(16) = 48$
7. $3 \times 8 + 2^3 = 3 \times 8 + 8 = 24 + 8 = 32$
8. $\sqrt{25 - 16} = \sqrt{9} = 3$
9. $\sqrt{25} - \sqrt{16} = 5 - 4 = 1$
10. $5 + 3(7 + 1) = 5 + 3(8) = 5 + 24 = 29$
11. $1 + 12 - 9 \div 3 \times 4 = 1 + 12 - 3 \times 4 = 1 + 12 - 12 = 1$
12. $3^2 + 7^2 = 9 + 49 = 58$

Lesson 6. Algebra

Practice Evaluating Expressions

1. $u + v = 5 + {}^{-}1 = 4$
2. $wx = (3)(0.4) = 1.2$
3. $w^2 = (3)^2 = (3)(3) = 9$
4. $xv = (0.4)({}^{-}1) = {}^{-}0.4$
5. $\dfrac{u}{x} = \dfrac{5}{0.4} = 12.5$
6. $w - v = 3 - {}^{-}1 = 3 + 1 = 4$
7. $w^2 + x = (3)^2 + 0.4 = (3)(3) + 0.4 = 9.4$
8. $(uv)w = ((5)({}^{-}1))(3) = ({}^{-}5)(3) = {}^{-}15$
9. $\dfrac{u}{v} - w = \dfrac{5}{-1} - 3 = {}^{-}5 - 3 = {}^{-}8$
10. $v^2 - x = ({}^{-}1)^2 - 0.4 = ({}^{-}1)({}^{-}1) - 0.4 = 1 - 0.4 = 0.6$
11. $5x + u = 5(0.4) + 5 = 2 + 5 = 7$
12. $2u - v = 2(5) - {}^{-}1 = 10 - {}^{-}1 = 10 + 1 = 11$

Practice Recognizing Properties

1. Commutative Property of Addition
2. Distributive Property
3. Commutative Property of Addition
4. Associative Property of Addition
5. Distributive Property
6. Associative Property of Multiplication

Practice Simplifying Expressions

1. $7p - 3p = 4p$
2. $(7p)(3p) = (7)(3)(p)(p) = 21p^2$
3. $x^2x^5 = x^{2+5} = x^7$
4. $9x^2 + 3x^2 = (9 + 3)x^2 = 12x^2$
5. $8(3x) = (8 \times 3)x = 24x$
6. $(y^2)^4 = y^{(2\times4)} = y^8$
7. $u^2 - v^2$ Cannot be simplified
8. $15x^5 - 11x^5 = (15 - 11)x^5 = 4x^5$
9. $(u^2v^3)^4 = (u^2)^4(v^3)^4 = u^{2\times4}v^{3\times4} = u^8v^{12}$
10. $6 - 2x$ Cannot be simplified
11. $5y^3 - y^3 = (5 - 1)y^3 = 4y^3$
12. $5x^2 + 4x$ Cannot be simplified

Practice Solving Equations

$$x - 13 = 0$$
1. $x - \underline{13+13} = \underline{0+13}$
$$x = 13$$

2. $$5x = 35$$
$$\frac{5x}{\underline{5}} = \frac{35}{\underline{5}}$$
$$x = 7$$

$$\frac{x}{4} = 6$$
3. $\underline{4}\left(\dfrac{x}{4}\right) = \underline{4}(6)$
$$x = 24$$

4.
$$3x - 7 = 5$$
$$3x - \underline{7+7} = \underline{5+7}$$
$$3x = 12$$
$$\frac{3x}{\underline{3}} = \frac{12}{\underline{3}}$$
$$x = 4$$

5.
$$5x + 1 = 16$$
$$5x + \underline{1-1} = \underline{16-1}$$
$$5x = 15$$
$$\frac{5x}{\underline{5}} = \frac{15}{\underline{5}}$$
$$x = 3$$

6.
$$2 + 5x = 12$$
$$\underline{2-2} + 5x = \underline{12-2}$$
$$5x = 10$$
$$\frac{5x}{\underline{5}} = \frac{10}{\underline{5}}$$
$$x = 2$$

7.
$$6 - 3x = {}^-3$$
$$6 - 3\underline{x+3x} = {}^-3\underline{+3x}$$
$$6 = {}^-3 + 3x$$
$$\underline{6+3} = {}^-3\underline{+3} + 3x$$
$$9 = 3x$$
$$3x = 9$$
$$\frac{3x}{\underline{3}} = \frac{9}{\underline{3}}$$
$$x = 3$$

8.
$$4x + 8 = 2x$$
$$4\underline{x-2x} + 8 = 2\underline{x-2x}$$
$$2x + 8 = 0$$
$$2x + 8\underline{-8} = 0\underline{-8}$$
$$2x = {}^-8$$
$$\frac{2x}{\underline{2}} = \frac{{}^-8}{\underline{2}}$$
$$x = {}^-4$$

9.
$$x + y = 5$$
$$x + y\underline{-y} = 5\underline{-y}$$
$$x = 5 - y$$

10.
$$4x - 3y = 12$$
$$4x - 3\underline{y+3y} = 12\underline{+3y}$$
$$4x = 12 + 3y$$
$$\frac{4x}{\underline{4}} = \frac{12}{\underline{4}} + \frac{3y}{\underline{4}}$$
$$x = 3 + \frac{3}{4}y$$

11.
$$\frac{2x}{3} + 1 = 15$$
$$\frac{2x}{3} + 1\underline{-1} = 15\underline{-1}$$
$$\frac{2x}{3} = 14$$
$$\underline{3}\left(\frac{2x}{3}\right) = \underline{3}(14)$$
$$2x = 42$$
$$\frac{2x}{\underline{2}} = \frac{42}{\underline{2}}$$
$$x = 21$$

12.
$$\frac{x}{2} + y = 7$$
$$\frac{x}{2} + y - y = 7 - y$$
$$\frac{x}{2} = 7 - y$$
$$2\left(\frac{x}{2}\right) = 2(7 - y)$$
$$x = 14 - 2y$$

Practice Solving Inequalities

1.
$$x - 5 < 7$$
$$x - 5\underline{+5} < 7\underline{+5}$$
$$x < 12$$

2.
$$2x + 4 > 2$$
$$2x + 4\underline{-4} > 2\underline{-4}$$
$$2x > {}^-2$$
$$\frac{2x}{\underline{2}} > \frac{{}^-2}{\underline{2}}$$
$$x > {}^-1$$

$$\frac{x}{3} \leq -5$$

3. $3\left(\frac{x}{3}\right) \leq 3(^-5)$

$$x \leq ^-15$$

4.
$$4 - 3x \geq 10$$
$$4-4 - 3x \geq 10-4$$
$$^-3x \geq 6$$
$$\frac{^-3x}{^-3} \leq \frac{6}{^-3}$$
$$x \leq ^-2$$

5.
$$10x \leq 5$$
$$\frac{10x}{10} \leq \frac{5}{10}$$
$$x \leq \frac{5}{10}$$
$$x \leq \frac{1}{2}$$

6.
$$^-x \geq ^-4$$
$$^-1x \geq ^-4$$
$$\frac{^-1x}{^-1} \leq \frac{^-4}{^-1}$$
$$x \leq 4$$

7.
$$5x - 7 < 18$$
$$5x - 7+7 < 18+7$$
$$5x < 25$$
$$\frac{5x}{5} < \frac{25}{5}$$
$$x < 5$$

8.
$$8 - 3x \leq 5$$
$$8-8 - 3x \leq 5-8$$
$$^-3x \leq ^-3$$
$$\frac{^-3x}{^-3} \geq \frac{^-3}{^-3}$$
$$x \geq 1$$

Lesson 7. Problem Solving

Practice Problem Solving

1. The problem asks for the amount of the tip. You are finding the *Part* in a percent problem. The *Whole* is 34 and the % is 15. *Part* = % × *Whole* ÷ 100 = 15 × 34 ÷ 100 = 5.1. The tip is $5.10.
2. The cost of a used textbook is 75% (100% − 25%) of the cost of a new one. The % is 75 and the *Part* is 36. You are looking for the *Whole* in a percent problem. *Whole* = *Part* ÷ % × 100 = 36 ÷ 75 × 100 = 48. The cost of a new text is $48.
3. The *amount* of the markup is $75 ($200 − $125). This is the Part in a percent problem. The Whole is the $125 that is being marked up. You are looking for the %. % = *Part* ÷ *Whole* × 100 = 75 ÷ 125 × 100 = 60. The jewelry is marked up 60%.
4. You are looking for the discounted amount. The discounted price is 80% (100% − 20%) of the retail price. This is the Part in a percent problem. The % is 80 and the whole is $62. *Part* = % × *Whole* ÷ 100 = 80 × 62 ÷ 100 = 49.6. The discounted price is $49.60.

5. The problem asks for a "clock time," but first you have to determine how long it will take Karen to drive 15 miles. Use the formula $t = \dfrac{d}{r} = \dfrac{15}{25} = 0.6$. The drive is 0.6 hour, or $0.6 \times 60 = 36$ minutes. Karen will have to leave at least 36 minutes before 2:30 or by 1:54 P.M.

6. You need to compare 450 miles with the distance Kenny can travel on a full tank of gas. This distance is $28 \times 18 = 504$ miles, so yes, he can make the trip on one tank.

7. Set up the proportion $\dfrac{19}{20} = \dfrac{x}{400}$. Then solve $x = 19 \times 400 \div 20 = 380$. J.J. could expect to make 380 free throws during the season.

8. The amount of the discount is $7. You are looking for the % in a percent problem in which the Whole is $35 and the Part is $7. % = *Part* ÷ *Whole* $\times 100 = 7 \div 35 \times 100 = 20$. The discount is 20%.

9. To determine gas mileage, divide miles by gallons. Sam got $90 \div 5.6 \approx 16.07$ miles per gallon. Ellen got $130 \div 6.1 \approx 21.31$ miles per gallon. Subtract to find how much better Ellen's gas mileage was than Sam's: $21.31 - 16.07 = 5.24$ miles per gallon.

10. First you have to find out how much the stock was sold per share: $800 \div 50 = 16 per share. The increase per share was $4 ($16 - 12). You are looking for % in a percent problem, where the Whole is $12 and the part is $4: % = *Part* ÷ *Whole* $\times 100 = 4 \div 12 \times 100 = 33\tfrac{1}{3}$. The value of the stock went up $33\tfrac{1}{3}$%.

Lesson 8. Applied Algebra

Practice Pattern

1. 16: Add 3 to each number to get the next number.
2. ⁻14: Subtract 5 from each number to get the next number.
3. 22: To get each number after the first, you added the following numbers in sequence: 1, 2, 3, 4, 5. Add 6 to 16 to get 22.
4. ⁻2: The signs alternate and the absolute values go down by 1.
5. ⁻14: Subtract 3 from each number to get the next number.
6. To get each number after the first, you added the next term in the sequence 3, 5, 7, 9. Add 11 to 26 to get 37.
7. To get each number after the first, you added the next term in the sequence 2, 4, 6, 8. Add 10 to get 23.
8. 22: Add 5 to each number to get the next number: $17 + 5 = 22$.
9. 54: Multiply each number by 3 to get the next number: $3 \times 18 = 54$.
10. To get each number after the first, subtract the next term in the sequence 1, 2, 3. The missing number is $0 - 4 = {}^-4$.

11.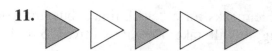

12.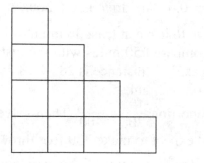

13.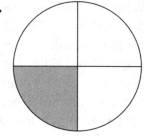

Practice Formula

1. There are 12 inches to a foot. Each inch is 2.54 centimeters, so there are $12 \times 2.54 = 30.48$ centimeters in a foot.

2. Substitute 150 for F in the formula: $C = \frac{5}{9}(150 - 32) \approx 65.6$. The equivalent Celsius temperature is 65.6°C.

3. Substitute 100 for P, 10 for t, and 0.03 for r in the formula $A = 100(1 + 0.03)^{10} \approx 134.39$. After 10 years, \$100 will be worth \$134.39.

4. First you have to change 15 minutes to $\frac{1}{4}$ of an hour. Since $d = rt$, $r = 36$, and $t = 4\frac{1}{4}$, $d = 36 \times 4\frac{1}{4} = 153$. Stuart drives 153 miles.

5. Kathy's car gets 22 miles per gallon, and the tank holds 15 gallons. She can drive $22 \times 15 = 330$ miles. Therefore she cannot make it to Phoenix on one tank.

6. The volume is 2 cubic centimeters and the mass is 38.6 grams. Substitute these in the formula to get $\frac{38.6}{2} = 19.3$. The density of gold is 19.3 grams per cubic centimeter.

7. Substitute 5 for x in the formula to get $I = \frac{100}{5^2} = \frac{100}{25} = 4$ lumens.

Practice Words to Symbols

1. $x + 10$
2. $10 > x$
3. $12x - 8$
4. $3(x + 5)$
5. $3x < 9$
6. $6x - 2 = 25$
7. $2(x + 5) > 50$
8. $3x - 10 \geq 15$
9. $x - 4 < 4$
10. $7(x + 5) \leq 50$

Lesson 9. Geometry

Practice Geometry Definitions

1. Figures A and C, because they have the same shape.
2. Figure C, because it has the same shape and size.
3. Figure D, because it has 4 equal sides.
4. Billy needs to cut out 2 circles the same size and one rectangle that has a width the same length as the circumference of the circle.

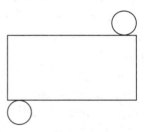

5. Is $(90 - 48)° = 43°$
6. Is $(180 - 55)° = 125°$
7. B, because the 2 figures have the same size and shape.
8. This is an isosceles triangle, because 2 sides are equal.
9. The diameter is twice the length of the radius, or 40 inches.
10. This is a tangent because it touches the circle in 1 point only.

Practice using Triangle Facts

1. The angles of a triangle add to make 180°. Add 50 and 35 to get 85, then subtract from 180° to get 95°.
2. The other base angle is also 40°. To get the third angle, subtract 80 $(40 + 40)$ from 180° or 100°.
3. According to the Pythagorean Theorem, the square of the hypotenuse is $6^2 + 8^2 = 36 + 64 = 100$. The length of the hypotenuse is $\sqrt{100} = 10$ meters.

4. Compare $4^2 + 6^2 = 16 + 36 = 52$ and $8^2 = 64$. Since $52 \neq 64$, the triangle is *not* a right triangle.

5. If a and b are the legs of a right triangle, and c is the hypotenuse, the Pythagorean Theorem says $a^2 + b^2 = c^2$. Substitute 12 for a and 15 for c to get $12^2 + b^2 = 15^2$, or $144 + b^2 = 225$. Solve this equation for b by subtracting 144 from both sides $144 - 144 + b^2 = 225 - 144$, or $b^2 = 81$, and taking $\sqrt{81} = 9$. The length of the other leg is 9 feet.

6. North and east are at right angles to each other, so these two distances are the legs of a right triangle. His distance from his starting point is the hypotenuse of this right triangle. Substitute 50 for a and 120 for b in the Pythagorean Theorem to get $c^2 = 50^2 + 120^2 = 16{,}900$, and take $\sqrt{16{,}900} = 130$. Matt is 130 feet from his starting point.

7. Add 95 and 40 to get 135, and subtract 135 from 180 to get 45° for the third angle. This is an *acute* angle.

Perimeter, Area, and Volume Practice

1. Volume of a box is length times width times height: $5 \times 2 \times 1 = 10$ cubic feet (ft^3).

2. The length of the pool is 51 feet. Divide by 3 to get yards: 17 yards.

3. The pool is a rectangular prism with dimension 51, 39, and 4. The volume is $51 \times 39 \times 4 = 7956$ cubic feet. This is the amount of water it will hold.

4. Divide the volume 7956 cubic feet by the filling rate 240, to get 33.15 hours to fill the pool.

5. The amount of edging she needs is the circumference of the circular garden. This is approximately $3.14 \times diameter = 47.1$ feet.

7. The area of a wall is its length times its height. Two of the walls have a length of 14 feet, and two have a length of 18 feet. All heights are 8 feet. The total area of the walls is $(2 \times 14 \times 8) + (2 \times 18 \times 8) = 512$ square feet (ft^2).

8. You will need $512 \div 200 = 2.56$ gallons of paint. You will have to buy 3 gallons.

9. A soda can has the shape of a cylinder. Substitute 4 for r and 18 for h in the formula for the volume of a cylinder: $V = \pi r^2 h = \pi(4)^2(18) = 288 \approx 9904.8$ cubic centimeters (cc).

10. You are looking for the area of a circle with a diameter of 50 meters. The radius of this circle is 25 meters. Substitute 25 for r in the formula for the area of a circle: $A = \pi r^2 = \pi(25)^2 = 625\pi \approx 1963.5$ square meters (m^2).

Lesson 10. Measurement

Measurement Practice

1. Divide 435 by 60 to get 7.25 hours (7 hours and 15 minutes).

2. Don takes 2 hours to pick $\frac{1}{3}$ acre of blueberries. It will take him twice as long, or 4 hours, to pick the remaining $\frac{2}{3}$ acre. If he takes an hour for lunch, it will be 5 hours before he's done. He will finish at 3:00.

3. The temperature rises 6°F to 0°F, and then it rises 13°F more. Altogether, the temperature rises 19°F.

4. One football field is 300 feet long. Divide 2460 by 300 to determine the length of the cruise ship as a number of football fields: $2460 \div 300 = 8.2$.

5. The endpoints of the segment are at $2\frac{3}{4}$ and $4\frac{1}{2}$. You could subtract to find the length but it may be easier to count up: 1 unit to $3\frac{3}{4}$ and $\frac{3}{4}$ units to $4\frac{1}{2}$, making the length of $\overline{BD}$ $1\frac{3}{4}$.

6. In 12 hours the patient will receive $12 \times 20 = 240$ milliliters. Since there are 1000 milliliters in a liter, 240 milliliters is 0.240 liter in 12 hours.

7. A kilogram is a thousand grams, so 2.34 kilograms is $2.34 \times 1000 = 2340$ grams.

8. There are 16 ounces to each pound. There are $50 \div 16 = 3.125$ pounds of laundry detergent in the container.

9. Substitute 20 for C in the formula: $F = \frac{9}{5}(20) + 32 = 68$. A 20°C reading is equal to a 68°F reading.

10. There are 4 quarts to a gallon and 2 pints to a quart. Therefore, there are 8 pints to a gallon. It will take $4.25 \times 8 = 34$ pints of paint to paint the first floor.

Lesson 11. Coordinate Geometry

Coordinate Geometry Practice

1. a: To get to A from the origin $(0, 0)$, you move 5 right and 7 up. Right and up are both positive, so the coordinates of A are $(5, 7)$.

2. c: The arca of $ABCD$ is its length times its width. There are 7 squares between D and A and 12 squares between A and B. Multiply these to get and area of 84 square units.

3. c: You have to check the location of each point. Of the four points, only $(^-3, 6)$ is outside the rectangle.

4. a: The perimeter of a rectangle is twice is length plus twice its width. The length and width of *ABCD* are 7 and 12, so the perimeter is $(2 \times 7) + (2 \times 12) = 38$ units.
5. b: There is a right angle at *X,* so the triangle is a right triangle.
6. The formula for the area of a triangle is $A = \frac{1}{2}bh$, where *b* is a base and *h* is the corresponding altitude. The base $\overline{ZX}$ is 10 units long, and the altitude $\overline{XY}$ is 5 units long. $A = \frac{1}{2}(10)(5) = 25$ square units.
7. b: To get to *Z* from the origin (0, 0), move 5 units left and 1 unit up. The coordinates of this point are $(-5, 1)$.
8. b: Most of the points on $\overline{XY}$ are right and below the origin (0, 0). Right means *x* is positive, and below means *y* is negative.

Lesson 12. Data Analysis

Practice Summarizing Data

1. To find the median, first put the numbers in order from smallest to largest: 26, 29, 35, 37, 38, 41, 42. The median is the middle number, 37.
2. There are 12 months in a year, so multiply 12 times 18.6 to get 223.2 reported car thefts per year.
3. To get the average of a set of numbers, you add the numbers and divide the total by the number of numbers. Chinn's total score on the four tests is $95 + 90 + 89 + 85 = 359$. To have an average of 90 on five tests, his total score would have to be $5 \times 90 = 450$. Therefore Chinn needs a score of $450 - 359 = 91$.
4. The median is the middle number when the numbers are in order from smallest to largest. In this case, the median is $803.27. This is still the middle number of the five when the largest number changes from $1,480 to $4,180. So the median is unchanged. To get the mean, add the numbers and divide by 5. The mean of the corrected numbers is much greater than the original mean because $4,180 is added instead of $1,480.
5. The modal category is "poodles" because it is the one with the greatest frequency.

Probability Practice

1. There are $35 + 28 = 63$ roses altogether and 35 are yellow. Therefore, the probability that Grace picks a yellow rose is $\frac{35}{63} = \frac{5}{9}$.
2. There are 8 numbers on the spinner and 2 of them are less than 3. The probability is $\frac{2}{8} = \frac{1}{4}$.
3. There are $13 + 18 = 31$ in the class altogether. Of these 18 are women. The probability is $\frac{18}{31}$.

4. There are $8 + 5 + 4 + 2 = 19$ M&Ms in the bag. Of these 4 are red. The probability is $\frac{4}{19}$.

5. On average, Lucas would make 88 of 100 free throws taken. This means that on average he would miss 12 of every 100. The probability is $\frac{12}{100} = \frac{3}{25}$.

Counting Problems Practice

1. There are $40 - 22 = 28$ men in the office.

2. If you add the number of Super Cola and sugar-free cola you get 112 cases altogether. You have to subtract the 13 cases of Super Cola that are also sugar free because those have been counted twice. The answer is 99 cases.

3. A Venn diagram is the best way to solve this problem.

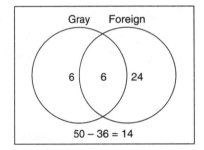

The circles represent gray cars and foreign cars. Gray foreign cars are represented by the intersection of the two circles, and there are 6 of these. There are also 6 gray American cars and 24 foreign cars that are not gray. Altogether, there are 36 cars that are gray or foreign. The portion of the Venn diagram outside both circles represents American cars that are not gray. Since there are 50 cars altogether, there are $50 - 36 = 14$ of these cars.

4. There are 6 fried items and 3 of these contain beef. The remaining 3 fried items do not contain beef.

INDEX